ISBN: 979-85-6228603-1

Copyright © Ana Elisa Miranda & Ute Limacher-Riebold 2020

All rights reserved. No part of this publication may be reproduced, stored in a retrieval system, distributed or transmitted in any form or by any means, including electronic, mechanical, photocopying, recording or otherwise, without prior permission in writing of the authors, except in the case of brief quotations embodied in critical reviews and certain other noncommercial uses permitted by copyright law. For permission requests, write to the authors Ana Elisa Miranda and Ute Limacher-Riebold, addressed "Attention: Permission Coordinator" at info@UtesInternationalLounge.com and / or anaelisasm@gmail.com

Cover design and edited by Ute Limacher-Riebold

The Toolbox

for Multilingual Families

Ana Elisa Miranda & Ute Limacher-Riebold

Table of Contents

Hi there! 1

Why we created *The Toolbox* 2

How to use *The Toolbox* 5

How to best support your family languages 8

Understanding and Speaking 12

    1. Imitating sounds 14

    2. Play with consonant-vowel combinations 14

    3. Singing 15

    4. Comment on gestures 15

    5. Pointing games 16

    6. The power of gestures and sounds 17

    7. Play with baby words 18

    8. Talking the talk 19

    9. Animal sounds 19

    10. Stretching words / Exploring words 20

    11. Reading Picture books 21

    12. Role Play 22

    13. A walk in nature 23

    14. Questions and answers 23

    15. All the colours of the rainbow 24

    16. Naming body parts 25

    17. Storytelling 26

    18. Finding the object 27

19. Guessing the object 28

20. Spot the difference 29

21. The syllable game 29

22. Singing with preschool and school-aged children 30

23. Sound- and Letter-chain 30

24. The syllable game (2) 31

25. Yes and no game 32

26. Board Games 33

27. Chinese Portraits 34

28. Don't say it... 36

29. Multi-Meaning Words 37

30. Charade or Catch Phrase 38

31. Aunt Mary 40

32. Picture Dictation 41

33. Card games (general) 41

34. Story Cubes 42

35. Water-Words 43

36. Password Game 43

37. Gibberish 45

38. I go on a trip and I pack... 46

39. Chinese Whispers 46

40. Word Family 47

41. One duck... 48

42. Compound words | Find the longest word 49

43. Toothless 50

44. Coded language 50

45. Can you count until 100? 51

46. Long Sentence — Memory game 52

47. Fight for attention 53

48. Association — Meaning game	53
49. Listen… — Find Word Patterns	54
50. Composing your own rap	55
51. Guess the language	56

Before picking up a book or a pencil… 57

52. Read aloud	57
53. I spy	58
54. Sorting Letter/Sounds	59
55. Rhyming Sentences	60
56. Making up characters	60
57. Odd one out	61
58. Tongue Twisters	61
59. Word Puzzle	62
60. Word Snake	62

Supporting motor skills development 64

61. Cooking	64
62. Building	65
63. Crafts	65
64. Drawing and colouring	66

Learning to Read and Write 68

Print — making sense of lines and curves 69

65. Name Crafts	69
66. Tactile Letters and Numbers	69
67. Signs and labels	70
68. Letter Hunt	70
69. Close reading	71
70. Eat them!	72

- 71. Environmental Print 73
- 72. Calendar/Routine chart 73
- 73. Parent - Child message board 74

Learning the code 75

- 74. Letter — Sound Matching 75
- 75. Touch and Feel 76
- 76. Alphabet Book 76
- 77. Little Writers 77
- 78. Word cards 79
- 79. Word games 80
- 80. Spelling Games 83
- 81. Decodable Books 83
- 82. Spelling Tricky Words 85

Understanding Text 88

- 83. Predicting 88
- 84. Inferring 89
- 85. Retelling 89
- 86. World knowledge 90
- 87. Mental Images 91
- 88. Summarizing 92
- 89. Word Choice Pockets 92
- 90. Word Web 93

Turning ideas into words 95

- 91. Building Sentences 95
- 92. Shared Writing 95
- 93. Recorded Writing 96
- 94. Dictation 97
- 95. Sequencing 97

    96. Expanding Sentences 98
    97. Text Puzzle 98
    98. Word Choice 99
    99. Questions and Answers 99

Working on Fluency 101
    100. Audiobooks 101
    101. Emotions 101
    102. Paired Reading 102
    103. Recorded Reading 103
    104. Drama 103
    105. Punctuation 104

Reading Motivation 105
    106. A Special Treat 105
    107. Reading Dates 105
    108. Library visits 106
    109. Organize your bookshelf 106
    110. Put the books down 107
    111. Reading Goals 108
    112. Book Swap 109
    113. Review and Rate 110
    114. Join a Book Club 110
    115. Watch Booktubers 111

Writing Motivation 112
    116. Cards 112
    117. Happiness Jar 112
    118. Toy Stories 113
    119. Stop Motion Video 114
    120. Read About Authors 114

121. Comics	115
122. Snail Mail	116
123. Journal or Scrapbook	116
THANK YOU!	**117**

Hi there!

I'm Ana. I've been a teacher for almost half of my life. I teach English as a Second Language and for the past five years I've been working as a learning support teacher at an international school. My absolute favorite thing to teach and learn about is the process of learning to read and write. That's why I recently completed a specialization in literacy and dyslexia. It's fascinating to watch that learning happens.

I love the multicultural environment I'm immersed in everyday, I get to learn about dozens of countries and share a bit about mine: Brazil.

I've lived in the USA, and now I call Belgium my home. It's where I met my partner and where we're raising our family — speaking Portuguese, Dutch, English and sometimes a little French.

I'm Ute. I grew up with multiple languages. I hold a PhD in Romance Philology and have taught linguistics at University level in Zurich (Switzerland). I support multilingual families in maintaining their family languages while learning new ones as an independent language consultant at *Ute's International Lounge*. I regularly hold workshops and trainings for parents, educators and health practitioners about multilingualism and raising children with multiple languages. I have also been teaching German, Italian and French to teenagers and adult advanced learners for more than 30 years. It is fascinating to observe the many ways we acquire and learn languages. After living in Italy, Switzerland and France, I now live in the Netherlands, but so far never in my country of origin, Germany. I thrive in international, multilingual and multicultural settings, as do my three teenage children who grow up with German, Swiss German, Dutch, English, Italian, French, and Spanish.

Why we created *The Toolbox*

"The limits of my language are the limits of my world." Ludwig Wittgenstein

We believe that learning languages opens the doors to the world. It gives us a unique perspective of cultures and people. It opens our minds and hearts to what is different.

Multilingualism is very common — more than half of the world's population speaks more than one language on a regular basis. Children all around the globe grow up speaking multiple languages and dialects. However, we know that not every family experiences a smooth process. Some are not supported by their relatives and community, some struggle to find resources and opportunities for minority language input, some are misinformed, while others even think their language is not relevant enough to pass on.

Whichever your situation might be at the moment, you can pass on your language to your children. They *can* learn to speak, read and write in different languages.

We created **The Toolbox** to guide you and inspire you with activities and games that foster **understanding, speaking, reading and writing**. We know that finding the right activity to encourage children to speak, read and write all their languages is not an easy task. For this *Toolbox* we have selected activities and games that parents, teachers and educators have used to foster language in different settings.

Understanding and speaking are natural processes in language *acquisition* and require mainly consistent exposure to the target language. We transmit our language to our children from day one by simply talking to them. From day one we communicate with our children and connect in non-verbal and verbal ways that are essential for our children's healthy development. Nevertheless, fostering a broader vocabulary in all our family languages requires us to create opportunities to explore different domains of life. Some of the activities that foster understanding and speaking, as well as phonological awareness, can easily be implemented into our daily routine. Others will require more time and preparation, and more people to engage in them, with a variety of levels of fluency in the target language.

Reading and writing require formal teaching. Some parents wait for their children to be taught reading and writing in the school language before teaching them in the family languages, as teachers have all the tools and strategies to support children's literacy skills. Moreover, reading and writing skills can be transferred to other languages and once children are confident enough in their school language, reading and writing in the other languages might be an easier process.

On the other hand, some parents are keen to teach their children to read and write in their family languages, either before or alongside school literacy instruction. These parents must be willing to take on a teacher's role — preparing themselves, choosing materials and activities, making time for instruction and practice.

Please bear in mind that every child is different. Some children are eager to learn how to read and write, others prefer to wait a bit longer. We encourage you to follow your children's lead and hope you find inspiring activities to foster all your family languages.

We are aware that there are many more activities in each language than those we chose for this *Toolbox*, and that some of those we share might not be suitable for every language and therefore need some adjustment. But we hope that with the activities and games we chose, we inspire you to explore, and maybe come up with a personal version of it.

Learning languages is a fantastic process that encourages resilience, patience, self-awareness, self-confidence, communication, creativity and so much more. It is an everyday choice and commitment. It might not always be easy, but absolutely worth it!

How to use *The Toolbox*

Our goal is to help multilingual families foster all their languages in a practical, engaging and fun way. *The Toolbox* provides parents and caregivers with ideas for activities that can be done one on one or in groups, and that can be adapted to your different family languages.

The activities are divided into sections. In the first section you find activities that foster **understanding** and **speaking**, for 0-15 year-old children who are acquiring their first languages or learning additional ones. In the two chapters **Before picking up a book or a pencil** and **Supporting motor skills development** we share activities that help children develop the necessary skills to learn how to read and write.

In the second section, we list activities that support **reading** and **writing**, and are rather aimed at preschool and school-aged children (3+ year-olds). Some of these might require more time and energy to prepare. They are organized in the following categories: **Print: making sense of lines and curves** — activities that introduce children to the written symbols of their language, **Learning the code** — when children begin to learn the basics of reading and writing, **Understanding text** — exercises to facilitate reading comprehension, **Turning ideas into words** — activities to help children develop writing skills, **Working on fluency** — activities that further develop reading skills, **Reading motivation** and **Writing**

motivation — ways to encourage your children to stay engaged and enjoy learning to read and write.

Age group: We indicate the **minimum age** that is required for the activity. But as you can do these activities in all your family languages and your child might have different levels of fluency in them, some of them might be slightly under the age of your child. If you are looking for activities that your children can do in an additional language, you may want to consider activities for younger children that might correspond to their current level of fluency.

Material: Some of the activities require materials that you might have at home, such as paper, pens, but also card games or board games. We suggest that you see what you have at home, consider swapping or borrowing, explore the local library, the consulate, embassy or cultural associations where you live, see if they can provide you with resources. Ask family, friends and in social media groups for books, games, free downloadables, printables. There are many online resources available, like ebooks, audiobooks, animations. You can also make your own. Make sure you choose age appropriate resources and use the electronic resources in an interactive way with your child.

Description: We explain the activity and give some examples that should be easily translatable and transferable to other languages.

Tips: You find alternatives for the activities and suggestions on how to use them with children from different age groups, different skills and levels of fluency.

We invite you to introduce *The Toolbox* activities to your children from an early age, so that using their languages with you, their siblings, extended family or friends becomes an enjoyable habit.

When choosing an activity, follow your children's skills and interests. Consider if your family's language goals are being met and how your children respond to it. The amount of guidance you provide versus how independently your children work will depend on their age and level in each language.

Feel free to modify the activities, create new ones, explore and do what works for your family!

How to best support your family languages

You have probably determined what your family languages are and what level of fluency your child needs to achieve in each one of them.

Successful language acquisition and learning require consistent quality exposure, which means that, ideally, your children would not only hear but also **use your languages on a regular basis**, preferably with more than one person.

This is what you can do daily to ensure that you and your children use your language in the most effective way. Choose the advice that is suitable for the age and language fluency of your children, and for the language goals you all aim at:

• Get used to speaking your language while doing daily routines — give explanations about what you do, how you do it, why, etc.
• Talk with your children in your language, take turns and discuss everyday topics and those your children are interested in.
• Listen to your children and give them enough time to talk, ask questions and explore your language.
• If your children struggle with finding the right words, encourage them to explain with words they know and help by modelling solutions.

- Invite your children to ask questions. If you struggle with finding answers, involve them in researching with you (eg. use age appropriate resources like a pictionary, dictionary, encyclopedia etc.).
- Explain and explore words that you use or your children need and want to know.
- Use your other languages in the presence of your children, in clear situations where these languages are necessary to guarantee effective communication. This will awaken their curiosity for languages and make them aware of social conventions related with language use.
- Use a variety of media to support your children's language development. Be sensible about age recommendations and discuss the choice and duration of each activity with them.
- Playful interactions stimulate the participation of children in any activity and learning process. Singing, playing finger rhymes, clapping hands, dancing, composing raps, and playing with languages make exploring and learning enjoyable.
- Exposure and repetition are crucial to learning a language! Children tend to want to repeat songs or stories over and over again.
- Use pictures in books, magazines etc. to talk about their content in the target language.
- Tell your children stories in your family languages.
- While playing games, engage your children in conversations about the topic.
- Start reading with your children as soon as possible: infants will learn that books tell stories, that stories are told following a certain structure,

and that pictures represent objects and actions that can be named and described with words.

• When reading picture books with preschool children, point to the objects and actions with your finger and later on, move your finger along the lines as you read: this will encourage them to try to decipher the words by themselves.

• Expose your children to printed materials in your language: books, magazines, games, posters, labels, etc.

• Have paper, writing materials and a surface readily available for your children to draw and write.

• Have movable letters to play with (eg. wooden, magnetic, sandpaper, foam, stickers, stamps).

• Listen to your children read once they start to learn. Choose appropriate books that they can read independently.

• Go to the library together.

• Make sure your children see you reading and writing with a purpose.

• Use your children's other interests to encourage reading and writing.

• If you want your children to read and write in your family languages:

- Set goals and make a plan together.
- Set aside regular time to work on the minority language.
- Use worksheets and workbooks in the target language.

During all activities and interactions with your children in where you focus on your languages, take your time and be understanding and relaxed.

Acquiring and learning languages require repetition, practice and making (many!) mistakes.

If you let your children use their imagination and play with the language, you nurture their creativity and confidence.

Do what you can, with what you have, and keep reflecting and tweaking in the process.

Understanding and Speaking

Understanding and starting to speak are natural processes, unlike reading and writing, which are processes that require formal learning.

When children acquire language, they first try to understand the sounds, their intonation, then they attempt to understand if sound-chains have a meaning. Later they understand that sound-chains can form a word that has a meaning and a function in a sentence, and that this meaning can vary depending on the context.

The shift from cooing to babbling, to saying words that people who are not family can understand, is a gradual process and requires time. Children develop in their own way and at their own pace. And when more than one or two languages are acquired and learned, we need to provide consistent input in each language and make sure these are used regularly, especially if the goal is for the children to develop their language skills more or less simultaneously.

Many studies have shown that there is a strong relation between how much we talk to our children and how fast they develop language skills. In the chapter **How to best support your family languages** you can find some basic daily habits parents should get into with their children to foster language understanding and speaking, and later reading and writing.

When the language our children hear is based on an activity or object that is engaging to them, a word or a phrase is more likely to be stored in their memory. There is also a greater opportunity to extend the talk when the children are engaged and play an active role. These diverse language experiences will provide children with greater exposure to different words which can increase vocabulary and overall understanding, not only of the meaning of words, but also the general use of the language: its intonation, when to use certain words and how to form words and sentences.

Understanding and speaking are skills we want our children to have in all their family languages. They might not develop equally, as it all depends on the input, the context we use the language, the time we can dedicate to fostering the language and the readiness of the child to understand and articulate the language.

The following activities are aimed at children from 0 to 15 years old. Even if you should decide to introduce an additional language later: you can! It is never too late! If you introduce an additional language to a school-aged child, you can start with activities for 9 months old onwards: in the **Tips** section of the activities you find suggestions on how to do these activities with older children.

1. Imitating sounds

Age group: 0-12 months

Description: As soon as your children utter sounds, reinforce their attempt by maintaining eye contact, and respond with speech. Imitate their vocalizations and try to emphasize the intonations, like raising the pitch of your voice to indicate a question.

If your other family language uses other intonations and pace in speech, make sure the person responsible for the other language does this activity too. It helps children acquire the "sound", the intonations used and the different pace of utterances in each language you speak with them.

2. Play with consonant-vowel combinations

Age group: 0+

Description: Model consonant and vowel syllables, like "papa" "mama" etc. by making eye contact, and praise your baby when they make an attempt to repeat the sounds, no matter how clear it is. Start with vowels like "a", "o" and then "e" and consonants like "c", "p", later "t" and "m". You can accompany this activity with gestures or baby sign language if you wish. Start with words of objects and people in the child's environment, or that the child can see or touch. It is important that you engage in this sound-playing interaction with your child as it will not only help to connect with your baby, but also lays the ground for communication which is an interaction made of turn takings. If your baby makes a sound while you change him, you can imitate that sound or change the intonation of it, for example.

3. Singing

Age group: 0+

Description: Make singing with your children a habit. Nursery rhymes help children recognize patterns of speech and learn vocabulary. Repeat as often as the children are up to it. Be aware that the attention span of babies and infants is short.

4. Comment on gestures

Age group: 5 months+

Description: Whenever your baby lifts their arm, stretches it, makes a fist, shows or hands you an object in their hands, make sure to not just take it or just thank your baby. Babies use gestures to communicate and get the attention of people around them. Through gestures they demonstrate their interest; they show what they want others to notice, or hold objects to communicate something. For babies, gestures are a way to start a conversation even before they become verbal.

Make it a game where you acknowledge the intent of the baby to engage in a conversation with you and comment, sound out what is happening! With infants: Expand on basic descriptions like "Let's put on your socks" and describe the object — ex. "These socks are so soft, they are green; and look, they are short!";

"That is a ball", "It is a very colourful ball: blue, red, green, yellow; and it bounces! Look how it bounces! Do you want us to play with it? Shall we let it roll?" Link it to other objects the infant knows "Look, the ball fits into the cup!" or their experience "We can play the ball with Anna!" Turn the infant's interest into a rich language development opportunity.

The activities below are also suitable for older children, and those who start understanding or speaking an additional language. Find more tips on how to adjust them to different age groups in the descriptions.

5. Pointing games

Age group: 9 months+

Description: Pointing games provide a rich language development opportunity for babies. These games are social and also include elements of turn taking and joint attention. Joint attention — sharing an interest with the children and focusing on the same activity — has been shown to be a critical element of language learning. The more an activity or object is engaging for the child, the more likely it is that the word or phrase will be stored in their memory. Diverse language experiences will provide children with greater exposure to different words which can increase vocabulary and understanding. It is important that parents complete their children's gestures like pointing at objects, pointing to get attention and pointing to indicate needs, with words: "Oh, you want me to give you the blue cup? Or the red cup? The blue one? Blue... like your sweater.". Furthermore, repeating key words will allow the children to make the connection between the sounds and the activity, object or emotion.

Tips: Pointing at objects is a way for infants to make others understand what they want and need, it can also lead them to prefer not making the effort to utter words that come with the gesture (like "Want" for "I want..." or "Look!..."). Always accompany your children's gesture with words and encourage other family members and friends to do the same.

6. The power of gestures and sounds

Age group: 9 months+

Description: Invite your baby/infant to imitate your actions like clapping hands, throwing kisses, waving goodbye, playing finger games, games like peek-a-boo, itsy-bitsy-spider and such. Use gestures with words as much as possible.

Each language has its own finger games.

Tips: Encourage family members who speak the other languages to play this kind of game with your baby. You can also sign up for *baby sign language* classes to add signs that you can use to emphasize specific words in all your family languages (like *milk*, *more*, *tired* etc.).

With older children you may want to focus on the gestures used in your language, the way one counts with fingers, waves, uses signs instead of words. The meaning of a sign or gesture can vary across cultures and languages, and mean the opposite of what you think. Make sure your children become aware of the variety of meanings a gesture can have.

7. Play with baby words

Age group: 10 months+

Description: If your children use baby words, use them only to indicate that you acknowledge their intention of communication and in contexts with words that other people understand. If your children say "wawa" (for water), you would repeat it once "You want *wawa?*" but then replace it with the word that others would understand: "Let's get you a cup of *water*" "Is the *water* not too cold?". Repeat the expected word in your language in a few other sentences so that your children hear it. Avoid correcting them.

Tips: Play with words in all your languages. Certain words might be easier to articulate in one language than the other. For example "acqua" (Italian for *water*) might be easier to pronounce — *aka* — than *water*. Acknowledge and encourage your children's attempt to say these words and repeat them whenever possible in other contexts.

8. Talking the talk

Age group: 0-2 years

Description: Talk and comment on everything you do, when you bathe, feed and dress your baby, talk about what you are doing, where you are going, what you do before you leave the house, what you will do when you come back, who and what you will see.

In order to foster everyday words in all your languages, make sure the activities you are commenting on are also done by the other people speaking the other languages.

Tips: Talking as much as you can in the target language will increase the exposure of your children to the language. Even if they are already verbal, speak already: keep on talking as much as you can in the target language with them. You might not comment on every single action, but talk about what you are thinking, what you are going to do, what objects you use for example for cooking, how you measure and count ingredients etc.

9. Animal sounds

Age group: 0-2 years

Description: Introduce animal sounds in your languages and explore how they differ, every time you play with animal toys or read books with animals, go to the zoo or see an animal.

Each language has specific animal sounds. The sheep for example says "bah" in English, but "mäh" in German, whereas the cow says "muuh" in

German which sounds like the English "moo" and Italian "mu". You can make it a game to explore animal sounds in all your family languages! Use songs like *Old McDonald had a farm*, CD's or Youtube videos to explore these sounds.

Tips: With preschool and school-aged children you can introduce how the animal sound is called, like "the dog barks / is barking", "the cat is meowing", "the cow is mooing" etc., and explore the words in all their languages!

10. Stretching words / Exploring words

Age group: 1+

Description: Every time your children use a single word and not a sentence yet, use this word in an expanded context. For example, if your children say "ball", you would say "It's a blue *ball*", "Shall we play *ball*?" etc., later you can use longer sentences like "This is a nice *ball*", "I like this blue *ball*", "Shall we play *ball* together?", "Would you like to play *ball*?", "Do you want to roll the *ball*?", "I like to throw the *ball*" etc.

Tips: Try to use the new words your children say in all your languages, so that they can expand their vocabulary with (more or less) the same words in all their family languages.

11. Reading Picture books

Age group: 0-2 years

Description: Make reading to and with your children a routine. Find 10 minutes every day to read a picture book together. Reading with infants consists of describing the pictures of a book without following the written words. For your baby, choose soft books. Pictures should not be too detailed and they should have many colours. Choose sturdy books with large colourful pictures.

Point at the pictures, model the name of the objects in the book and encourage your infants to name the objects by asking them "what's this?". Make sure to adapt your pace to your children's. They might prefer staying on a page a bit longer or want you to repeat words several times. Take your time and listen to what your children have to say.

Tips: The advantage of picture books is that you can read them easily in all languages! There might be some pictures or items represented that are not easily translatable into your other languages, so make sure you have a look at the book before reading it and have the time to find the right words in your language. It helps you avoid frustration when searching for the right word or expression.

Older siblings who can't read yet, can *read* picture books to their baby brothers and sisters, and school-aged children can explore vocabulary they already know by trying to find the equivalent of the words in the additional language.

12. Role Play

Age group: 2+

Material: your imagination, dress-up clothes, toys, natural materials (sticks, stones, mud, etc.), things around the house

Description: This is an activity that develops children's imagination, oral language skills, vocabulary, storytelling and more.

Engage with your children's play and act out, try to extend the conversation — are you selling ice-cream, mud pies or fairy drinks? Are you kings and queens? Police and robber? Mom and baby? Doctor and patient? Are you having a party? — Why not act out your favourite stories? — Your children can also do role plays with siblings, friends and toys.

Tips: You can use role play to support a language that your children are (still) reluctant to speak. By assigning a specific language to a hand puppet, your children might be more prone to use the target language during the play.

Older children can combine the change of roles with the change of language, and try out simple sentences in the additional languages in a playful manner. You can help them by first providing input (eg. the necessary vocabulary) in the target language, and encourage them to use simple and short sentences that they can increase with time. Re-enacting something they experienced, a story they read, or a video or movie they watched, will help them process the situation and the acquired vocabulary in a fun way.

13. A walk in nature

Age group: 2+

Material: the environment around you

Description: When possible, go on a walk in nature with your children and encourage them to observe. What's the weather like? How have the seasons changed? Talk about what you see, hear, smell and feel.
Collect sticks, stones, seashells, flowers, leaves, nuts, seeds, etc. These can be used for play, building, arts and crafts and whatever else you can imagine.

Tips: Older children can do this activity with additional languages, by exploring names they might know in their other languages, finding out similarities and differences. Make sure it doesn't become a "lesson in nature" if the children are not ready for it. Learning to use an additional language takes time and patience, and many walks in nature!

14. Questions and answers

Age group: 2+

Description: With this activity your children will learn how open questions work, that they need to answer them with longer sentences, and that a simple "yes" or "no" won't suffice. For example, you would ask questions that require a choice, like "Do you want an apple or an orange?", "Do you want to wear the red or the blue shoes?".

If your children point instead of uttering the word, repeat the word and make eye contact (or physical contact by laying a hand on their shoulder or arm) and direct their attention to your mouth while repeating the word you would like them to try to articulate.

Tips: If your children have already learned to use open questions in their other languages, trying to formulate them in the target language might require some guidance: how do you ask questions in French, what are the rules when asking open questions in German etc.

With school-aged children it might be helpful to write them on a board or use cards to compare the different ways to ask questions in all your languages. Furthermore, you can prepare some standard ways to respond to open questions, like "I would rather like / take / use….", "I prefer using / taking / keeping…", "I think…", "I consider…".

Make sure to play this game in all your languages!

15. All the colours of the rainbow

Age group: 2-4

Material: pictures and objects around you

Description: Introduce colours and name them every time you use an object, look at a picture or see your children playing with something. You can let your children group toys per colour or find objects that have the same colour in your home.

When you introduce a new colour and you see that your children struggle with memorizing and pronouncing the word, use it in different contexts in the following days, and repeat this activity after 3 to 5 days. Help your children acquire those words in the other family languages too. It might take longer for them to articulate words that are more complicated for their current stage of language development.

Tips: Children growing up with multiple languages don't automatically know the colours in each of their languages! You can invite older children to describe pictures in a magazine, a book or on posters. Let them discover the different shades of colours in the target language, like *azzurro*, *blu*, *celeste* etc. in Italian or the different shades of *pink*, *fuchsia*, *purple* in English. You will experience that colours have different names and nuances in other languages and that what one considers *turquoise* is *verde acqua* for the other! **Knowing multiple languages allows us to see the world through faceted lenses!**

16. Naming body parts

Age group: 2-4

Description: This activity is about naming body parts. You can use a song like *Head, shoulders, knees and toes,* or other songs in your language, and touch the body part when you name it.

Tips: Expand this game by naming the body parts and telling what they can do: "my legs help me to walk", "with my hands I can wave, eat, clap…".

With school-aged children you can explore the details of each body part, how the bones are called, the muscles: you can make it an activity about human anatomy and biology.

Most multilinguals struggle with naming body parts and the actions related to them in all their languages. You may want to join in to play this game and learn some more words — you can explore which of the words in your languages are similar, and which ones differ the most.

17. Storytelling

Age group: 3+

Material: your imagination, puppets, props, writing material, recording devices, apps

Description: Telling a story can be as simple as describing what you did on a certain day, and as elaborate as putting on a puppet show, writing a book or making a stop-motion video.

Let's focus on oral storytelling. There might be many opportunities in a day to model, engage and encourage your children to tell stories:

— As you get ready in the morning or have breakfast, talk about a dream you had or what the plans for the day are.

— Having a visual daily chart is a great way for children to develop a sense of routine and sequence.

— As you role-play, read a book or build something together, encourage your children to describe and explain what they're doing.

— Remember past events: whenever you get a chance to connect with a memory, take it. See how your children remember and retell that day you went to the aquarium, the dentist, a birthday party or grandma's house. Share what you remember and ask them questions to keep it going.

— At the end of the day, share how everyone's day was.

Tips: Storytelling is a very important skill for everyone! Many adults struggle with telling stories in a compelling and interesting way. If you have made it a habit to tell stories in one of your family languages, make sure to make time for it in your other languages too! If your children are learning an additional language, let them start with the basic format and help them with formulating the beginning, middle and ending of stories. With older children you can explore sequencing by focussing on words like: *first*, *then*, *after that*, *in the end*, *finally*, *eventually* etc. (see the activity **Sequencing**). You can find templates online by searching "writing stories with children" in your languages.

18. Finding the object

Age group: 4+

Material: toys, pictures, anything that can be grouped together for this game

Description: Gather all kinds of toys or objects in one place (on the carpet or table) and choose one without telling your child. Now your child needs to guess which toy or object you chose by asking questions. "Does it have eyes?" "Is it red?" "Does it have wings?".

Tips: Alternatively, you can use pictures in magazines, books, on posters etc. Older children can play this game in their additional languages. They can start with easy objects and make it increasingly challenging.

19. Guessing the object

Age group: 4+

Material: toys, objects that your child knows and regularly uses (cup, spoon etc.)

Description: Place a series of objects or toys your child knows under a blanket (or in a huge bag). Make sure they don't see which objects you are hiding. Ask them to touch the hidden objects and describe what they feel and let them explore it. Help them to use and find words that describe the shape (round, edgy, big, small etc.), the material (soft, fluffy, hard, smooth etc.) and how it feels (nice, cold, warm, sticky etc.). The aim of this game is for your child to describe the object through touching it and guessing what it is.

Tips: You can also put all the toys or objects in a box or bowl, and instead of hiding them under a blanket, blindfold your children and let them either describe the object by exploring its shape, or you ask them to find for example the cow, the pencil, the button etc. If you play this game with younger or older children, make sure to adapt the objects to their age group. Play this game in each of your languages and explore the words — *cold* (English) and *kalt* (German) sound and mean the same, whereas *caldo* (Italian) sounds similar but means the opposite (warm)!

20. Spot the difference

Age group: 4+

Material: two almost identical pictures (you can find them online: "find/spot the difference")

Description: The goal is to compare two pictures that seem identical, and find a number of small differences.

Tips: It can be played alone and the results can be shared orally with others, or you can play it in groups of two or more, which makes finding the differences more interactive.

21. The syllable game

Age group: 4+

Description: The aim of the game is to count syllables, like in names, "John" (1 syllable), "Tho-mas" (2 syllables), "E-li-za-beth" (4 syllables), by clapping after every syllable. You can count syllables in rhymes or songs, emphasizing the stressed syllables by clapping or other physical movements (eg. tapping, jumping), as well as everyday sentences. Younger children can clap at every number in sentences like "one cup, two cups, three cups, four cups..." by taking turns or clapping at every number.
— It can be played with all kinds of rhymes, "Eeny, Meeny, Miney, Mo", "Please Porridge Hot" etc.

Tips: This game helps children become aware of the syllable structure of words also in additional languages. Instead of clapping hands, they can use drum sticks, or jump at each syllable, or take a step forward. Older children can try to make a rap out of the rhyming words. — Find online resources for "rhyming words" in several languages.

22. Singing with preschool and school-aged children

Age group: 5+

Description: You may have made singing a habit already. Preschool and school-aged children become able to recognize patterns of speech through singing. By spelling out words following the rhythm of the song or clapping hands for each syllable, children learn about the structure of words.

Tips: Every language has songs that help children to learn vocabulary, intonation, sentence structure and syllable structure. By playing this game in more than one language, your children will become aware of these differences between languages. Make sure to choose songs with words your children are familiar with or that they can put in a context.

23. Sound- and Letter-chain

Age group: 5+

Description: You can play this game everywhere, while traveling, at home etc. The first player says a word, for example "apple", the second player needs to find a word that starts with the last **sound**: /l/ like "lost". The next word needs to start with a /t/ and so forth.

Be aware that if you play it in French for example, focusing on **sounds**, the word "**eau**" (/o/) could prompt your child to choose "**au**to". In German, "Kind**er**" (pronounced with a final /a/) might prompt "**A**uto" etc.

Tips: With school-aged children you can focus on the last **letter** of the words, which will focus on spelling. You can also choose to only use specific **word categories** like nouns, verbs, or adjectives, only **names** (Sarah, Hanna, Anne etc.) or **follow a theme** (*Star Wars*; sweets; fruits; animals etc.)

In order to make it more challenging for older children, you can ask them to think of two words in a row, like "Eime**r** + **R**ad", "Drach**e** + **E**lefant", or add a time limit to find new words to add to the word chain.

This game can be played in different languages. You can also switch languages at each or every second or third turn.

If your children are learning an additional language and can already read, it might be helpful to use a list of words to play this game. Especially if they don't use the target language as frequently. Start with names, themes, or specific categories that they know some words already.

24. The syllable game (2)

Age group: 6+

Description: Choose any topic to find words to count syllables in. Start with two syllable words and increase the length of the word and the pace of the game. Count the fingers at every syllable, starting with the thumb for the first syllable (or another finger, depending on the language and habit in your culture when counting) and leave the fingers up until the counting is completed.

Tips: Older children can play this game in the additional language or combine words they know in another language with those in the new, target language. Invite them to take turns and make it a challenge of who can find the longest word. Another way to play this in multilingual families is to compare the length of a sentence in both languages based on how many syllables they have. This way your children will learn how to say the same thing in all the family languages and become aware of which language things can be said "faster" or "easier" in.

25. Yes and no game

Age group: 6+

Description: With this game, children learn how to understand and ask questions. Ask questions they would agree or disagree with, like: "Are you a car?", "Are you Anna?", "Do you want to eat the cup?", "Can a dog fly?" The aim of this game is to avoid answering *yes* or *no*.

After "Are you a car?" one can reply "I am not an object". To "Are you a bee?" one can reply "I have two legs" etc.

By asking questions quickly one after the other, the other player might slip a "yes" or a "no". If this happens, it's their turn to play and ask questions.

Tips: For older children you can ask questions like:

"Do you like maths/history/literature/sports/football/hockey….?"

"Is your sister/brother older than you?"

"Do you like watching movies on Youtube?"

You can also determine words that are not allowed to be said, like "nicht" (German) or "don't", "parce que" (French) etc. Adapt it to the language fluency level of the players.

If players are at different levels of fluency, one option can be to determine that those who are 10 years and older are not allowed to use "not", whereas those who are younger than 10 should avoid saying *yes* and *no*. You can make this game more difficult for older children by determining 3-4 words that need to be avoided.

For children to play this game in their additional language, they need to be able to form longer sentences and know how to avoid replying *yes* and *no* to a question.

Let children explore silly names, objects and concepts, and if they run out of words and they can already read, invite them to use a dictionary, thesaurus or encyclopedia. This is a fun game to play with older teenagers and adults as well. You may want to join the game and learn some new words too!

26. Board Games

Age group: 6+

Material: any board game

Description: All board games are tailored to facilitate communication and connection, and are suited to foster grammar and vocabulary. They also allow us to work on our communication skills, letting each other share their thoughts, reflections, and develop negotiating skills. You can play any kind of board game and adapt it to the players' age group, preferring the easier version if there is a big age difference.

Although all board games come with rules, allow some changes, add new rules, or find other ways to play them with your children. When negotiating the changes and the rules, you can foster your children's negotiating skills in the target language.

Tips: You can play board games in all your languages. For games with terms and references to a specific culture and language, explore how things, names, places etc. are called in your other languages.

If your children are learning an additional language, they might need some time to feel comfortable negotiating in it.

Most instructions come in different languages. If the target language is not among them, try to find the translation online. Your children can first read the instructions in the more familiar language and then try also in the target language. — Playing games should be fun and enjoyable, so make sure they don't feel pressured to play in the target language consistently. Let them lead the way!

27. Chinese Portraits

Age group: 6+

Material: pictures, paintings, photographs

Description: The goal of this game is to start from what is portrayed in a picture, painting, or photograph and to encourage the child's imagination by starting a conversation like: *If I was an animal/ a plant/ a season... a country/ a city / a planet / a car/ a colour / a book / a movie / a famous person / a dish / a fruit / a drink / a game / a number / a sport ..., I would be a ...* with the intention to foster vocabulary in all sorts of domains.

For example, if children respond "If I were an animal I would be a ***tiger***", ask what makes them choose to be a *tiger*. Help them find ways to describe characteristics of a tiger like: "brave", "courageous", "beautiful", "strong"... — Avoid suggesting solutions.

You can add as many questions as you want. Make sure to have fun and explore the vocabulary.

Tips: This game can be played in all your family languages and you can compare the answers in the different languages: what is the same, what is different?

If your children struggle with finding words in one language, instead of suggesting the solution, ask questions like "can the animal swim/fly...; in what country can we find this animal...; can you describe what this animal does/looks like..." and "what is this animal called in your *other* language(s)" etc.

As an option for older children you can alternate or change the language per player to make it multilingual and use all your languages in one game. For example, one player would ask questions in Italian and would ask the others to reply in Italian, the next player would ask the questions in French, the following one in German etc. This way your family could explore all your family languages.

If your children are still learning the target language, they will need some help with this game. Choose pictures that require a vocabulary at their level of fluency, or slightly above. Exploring up to 5 new words is feasible, but follow your children's lead in this.

28. Don't say it...

Age group: 6+

Material: cards or DIY images from magazines and books, paper, pen, timer

Description: This game is great to develop and expand the vocabulary. Similar to the *Taboo* game, players have to describe an object without using certain words, in a given time frame. Like describing a *tree* without using words like *plant*, *stem*, *branches*. Depending on the children's level of fluency, when describing a *balloon* they wouldn't be allowed to use *bursting*, *inflate*, *blow*, *float*.

Tips: Instead of words that can't be used to describe an object or word of your choice, you can ask the players to not use words starting with a certain letter, or that they have to avoid pronouncing certain sounds while responding. For example, if the word is *glass*: you could ask them to not say any word starting with a "t" like in "transparent" etc. When playing this game in languages your children are less fluent in, adjust the rules to their level of fluency.

For your older children to play this game in an additional language, they need to be able to know synonyms and be able to describe objects with other words. If they struggle, choose easier cards or images.

29. Multi-Meaning Words

Age group: 6+

Material: list of multi-meaning words in your family languages

Description: You play this game in groups of two or more. Unlike the *Yes and no game*, the aim in this game is for players to find multi-meaning words, like *organ* (the instrument and the part of the body) or *wave* (electric and water) etc. — The German name for this game is *Teekesselchen*.

One person chooses a multi-meaning word that the other players need to find out by asking questions that can only be answered with *yes* or *no*.

With younger children you can give a hint at the beginning of this game by saying for example "My word makes sounds". The other player then guesses for example: "Is it an instrument?" to which the first player will answer yes or no.

The person that is the fastest to find the word gets a point and/or gets to choose the next multi-meaning word.

Tips: You can prepare multi-meaning words in all your family languages and colour code them in order for players to choose which language they want to play in, or you can alternate languages in this game by switching between the word lists at every turn.

You can play this game in groups of two or more, or you can form two groups. For your children to play this game in an additional language, they need to have advanced language skills and be able to read in the target language, as they might want to use lists of words on- or offline to complete the tasks.

Here are some multi-meaning words in English:

bark, bat, bear, before, bill, blue, bore, bowl, brush, change, chest, clear, coat, cold, count, ear, fan, fence, fork, game, glasses, handle, head, jerk, kind, leaves, light, log, mine, mold, note, orange, paste, plain, organ, pool, pound, pupil, racket, range, rent, right, rose, saw, scale, shed, ship, sole, space, spring, squash, stable, steer, stern, stoop, store, train, trunk, watch, wave, well, yard etc.

If you google *multi-meaning words*, you can find many lists and pictures in different languages.

Like in the **Password Game** you can print or write all the multi-meaning words and collect them in a bowl or hat for players to draw from, or you can ask them to come up with words themselves.

30. Charade or Catch Phrase

Age group: 6+

Material: words or phrases to guess, written on strips of paper or generated by an *online word generator* and a timer

Description: This is a game that is more fun if played with more than 3 players. The aim of the game is to get your team members to guess the target word by explaining it to them without saying it or using any variant of it. You can prepare words and/or phrases beforehand, put them into a bowl or hat and divide the players into two teams.

The first player draws a word and shows it to the opposite team. He or she begins to describe, setting a timer (you can choose the length of the turns) and the team members start guessing while the opposing team stays quiet and watches the timer.

In this game, speed is the key. The goal is for players to get through as many words as they can before the timer runs out. For each guessed word the team gets one point. When the time is over, the bowl is passed to the other team.

Tips: If you want your children to use longer sentences, you can set a rule that the descriptions need to be full sentences. For example, if the word is "snowman", instead of "Frosty the..." they would need to say things like "It's something that is built in the winter in the shape of a human...". Also, if your goal is exploring vocabulary, you may want to set the timer a bit longer.

You can allow younger children to use shorter sentences. Should they not know the word, they can pass and choose the next one. If your children want to play this game in their additional language, make sure to adapt it to their level of fluency.

Another option is to let players describe the word in language A by using the language B. It would not be allowed to say the translation of the word or phrase though!

31. Aunt Mary

Age group: 6+

Description: This is a group game. — The first player talks to the person next to him: "Did you hear?" "What?" "Aunt Mary went shopping!" "What did she buy?" "An apple" — and player 1 will do as if he would eat an apple. The second player now continues the conversation with the 3rd player, also doing as if he was eating an apple. The dialogue is repeated until the last player is also doing as if he was eating an apple. In the next round, the first player will introduce another element and action, like "brushing the teeth". All the players will continue the movement or action prompted by the dialogue.

The effect is that while some of the players will still be doing as if they were eating an apple, the others will "brush their teeth" / "drink tea" / "iron the shirt" etc.

This game is suitable for children who like to move. You can choose to set some rules about the activities to prompt, like "sports" or "in the kitchen..." etc.

Tips: This game can be played in all languages. Depending on your children's level of fluency, the dialogue can be more or less elaborated. The combination of words and gestures makes it fun.

32. Picture Dictation

Age group: 7+

Material: pictures

Description: One player looks at a picture that the other player doesn't see and tries to describe it as detailed as possible while the other draws it. Through this game, children learn how to give more precise and detailed directions.

Tips: If your children play this game in their additional language, they may want to choose pictures that are at their level of fluency, i.e. that represent objects, actions etc. they can describe. This game can also be played in groups.

33. Card games (general)

Age group: 8+

Material: a deck of cards: traditional cards, *jass cards* (Switzerland), *Uno*, *Ligretto* etc.

Description: Any kind of card game can be adapted to the players' age group and to all the languages.

Some games might seem difficult to play in another language — like the Swiss German *Jass* where we use a specific Swiss German terminology and set of cards — but you can come up with new names in the *other* language you play it. The Swiss German *Tschau Sepp* has similar rules like the *Uno* card game, or *Mao Mao*, *Pumba*, *Makao*.

You can be inventive with the rules: alternate for example the colours to lay down on the table etc.

There are card games for every age group. For younger children you can choose *Snap*, *Old Maid*, *Go Fish*, *Slap Jack*, *Top Trump* etc.

Tips: Variations of many card games can be found in different cultures. It is interesting for our children to explore the different rules and ways to play them using different languages! The main intention with playing card games in multiple languages is to set the rules about what languages to use, talk about tactics and connect with the players in the target language.

34. Story Cubes

Age group: 6+

Material: Story Cubes (there are many varieties), or self made story cubes, pictures or memory cards.

Description: The Story Cubes game consists of nine dice with different pictures on each face. In turns, each player throws all the dice and tries to tell a story using all the pictures that are face up. You can choose to do this orally, and foster the children's vocabulary and storytelling skills. Or after telling the story, you help them draw it like a comic or write it down. Instead of the Story Cubes you can use pictures of objects or memory cards. You let your child choose the cards randomly and put them in a sequence that will help your child to structure the story. Don't focus too much on accuracy, but rather on content and enjoyment.

35. Water-Words

Age group: 8+

Description: Although similar to **Word Family**, and **Letter Chain** in this game players are asked to explore how many words can be formed with *water*: *waterfall, watermelon, waterman, waterloo, waterlog, watercolour, waterproof, mouthwatering, underwater, floodwater* etc.

You can compare the words in your different languages and explore if there are similarities in meaning.

Tips: Play the same game with words like *air, fire, land* which are words that can be found in all the languages. By exploring what compounds are possible in your children's additional languages, they will gain a greater insight into what unites languages (and cultures).

36. Password Game

Age group: 8+

Material: a list of words

Description: You can play this game in two or more teams, with two or more players per team. Players take turns writing 5 to 10 words on individual slips of paper. These words become the *passwords* used during the game.

Each team selects a player for each round, who picks a *password* from the opposite team's word bank. The player describes the term giving a one-word clue and the teammates have to guess the word first by taking turns giving one-word clues.

For example, if the word is "key", one can say "lock". If the other team doesn't guess the right password, it's the turn of the second team and so forth, until the password is found.

The team that guesses the password gets a point. If you play with two teams only, you would keep on giving one-word clues until the word is found.

To describe the password you can use nouns, verbs, adjectives, like "metal", "unlock", "cold" etc..

You can use online word generators as a resource for words. If you use multi-meaning words like *organ* or *wave*, the clue-givers can say any one-word clue they want, even if they use a different definition of the password that has previously been used. The same goes for words like *coach* or *bruise* that can be either verbs or nouns.

Tips: When playing this game in additional languages, your children can explore similarities and differences. Especially when playing the game in two groups and using different languages, this can be a very engaging game!

37. Gibberish

Age group: 8+

Material: a list of words or phrases

Description: This game allows children to explore how they can make themselves understood if they can't speak the additional language (yet), and is best played in a group. You give an instruction to the first player who needs to mime it. The goal is for the other participants to understand what he/she wants to say. The player is allowed to speak gibberish, i.e. by using intonation and sounds that are not any of his or her languages, and is allowed to use gestures.

Players can use any kind of aids to convey their message, as far as it is not writing the solution on a paper or device. Once the term or phrase has been guessed, it's the second players' turn and so on. The player who managed to get his message across the fastest wins.

Tips: By letting participants choose the language they want to play in, you give this game a multilingual twist, as the other players will also need to guess the other language based on the intonation and the gestures used.

An interesting part of this game is to find out that gestures can have different meanings in different languages.

38. I go on a trip and I pack...

Age group: 8+

Description: This game is funnier when several players participate. The first player says something like "I go on a trip and I pack a towel", the second player repeats the first and adds a second item, the third adds a third item and so forth. The player who doesn't remember one of the items will not continue participating in the game. The game ends when there is only one player left.

If the children don't know how an item is called in one of their languages, they can use a pictionary or ask other players for help.

Tips: For children to play this game in their additional language, they need to know the vocabulary related to packing a suitcase and going on a trip. Older children who are more fluent in more than one or two languages, can use terms from their different languages, for example "valise" (suitcase), "broek" (trousers) etc. If you notice that a player struggles with memorizing the different items in the language of the game, you can allow him/her to draw them on a paper or whiteboard.

39. Chinese Whispers

Age group: 10+

Description: For this game you need more players: the more the merrier! Players form a line. The first player comes up with a message and whispers it to the ear of the second person in the line. The second player whispers the message to the third player and so on. The last player will announce the message to the entire group and the first player will compare the original message with the final version. This game shows how errors can accumulate by retelling the message. The focus should be on the amusing and humorous effect of the message changing.

Tips: When playing this game in an additional language, children should make sure that those who are less fluent are at the beginning of the line, as it can be quite frustrating to be among those who "mess it all up" at the end! Also, the sentences shared should be understandable and, if necessary, you may want to slightly adjust the rules and allow a beginner to ask the person who is whispering, to repeat once (or twice).

40. Word Family

Age group: 10+

Material: list of words, timer

Description: Starting from a word that is chosen randomly from a list or a dictionary, each group has to find as many words that are associated with it or that are formed with it. For example "car": *cablecar, carwash*, but also *scarf,* and *Audi, Ford, wheels, gears* etc. The group that gathers most words in the set time, wins.

Tips: You can adapt the rules to any age group, level of fluency and language. For languages like German, which have many compounds, you can up the game by challenging players to find the longest words, or, on the contrary, avoid long words and focus more on the semantic field of a word, i.e. other words that are associated with the one the group chose.

41. One duck...

Age group: 10+

Description: The first player starts a sentence like "The duck with two legs jumps into the water, splash" (German: *Eine Ente, mit zwei Beinen, springt ins Wasser, plumps!*), where every player says part of the sentence: player 1: *One duck*, player 2: *with two legs*; player 3: *jumps into the water*; player 4: *splash!*, then it goes "Two ducks | with 4 legs | jump into the water | splash, splash", "Three ducks | with 6 legs |...." The number of "splash" increases with the number of ducks, so the first round only one player would say "splash", but in the second round two players would say it and so on.

At every turn, the number of ducks increases, as well as the legs and the players saying "splash". — How many ducks can you form this sentence with in the group, before making a mistake?

Tips: You can change the animal (times table) and choose an animal with 4 legs. You can also choose to count legs and wings, or legs and ears (six times table), or count legs, wings and ears of two different animals...

When playing this game in an additional language, your children might need an aid for the numbers, especially when switching to a language where numbers are inverted or follow another system — like English *seventy four* (70—4), German *vierundsiebzig* (4—70), or French *soixante quatorze* (60—14), unless they know them already.

42. Compound words I Find the longest word

Age group: 10+

Description: You can use picture memory cards or any picture (from a book or magazine) that you have previously chosen to form compound words. For example, you can use a memory card with a flower on it and ask your children to form all kinds of compound words with "flower". You can also let the children draw the two parts of a compound word — like drawing a sun and a flower to form: *sunflower*. Or you choose a random word and ask your children to find words that are compounds, like *ladybug, textbook, housekeeper, underwear* etc. If one of your family languages is German, you will find more words to play with, like *Pferdefuss, Pferdekuss, Bärentatze, Bienenstich, Mausefalle, Laufkatze, Hundehütte* etc.

For languages that don't have the same kind of compounds like German, you can allow compounds that are written with a hyphen, like *mother-in-law*, and compound adjectives, like *three-storey, one-way, short-term, easy-going, long-lasting, family-friendly, middle-aged, well-known, ready-made* etc. You can give this game an additional twist by comparing the spelling and grammar rules for the languages you speak at home.

Tips: If your children play this game in the additional language, they might need to use a dictionary.

43. Toothless

Age group: 10+

Description: In this game players ask questions and the aim is for participants to answer them without showing teeth. It is also not allowed to laugh. The person who manages to stay serious the longest, wins.

Tips: You can also play this game by asking players to avoid certain letters. For example: one player asks "Where do you live... but don't say the *b's*" and the other player needs to answer "I live in *'erlin* (Berlin)". Furthermore, instead of having a Question & Answer game, you can hold a whole conversation by avoiding pronouncing certain sounds.

44. Coded language

Age group: 10+

Description: Players talk to each other in a coded language, i.e. they intentionally insert a letter or syllable after each syllable, like **ba** "I**ba** am**ba** play**ba**ing**ba** foot**ba**ball**ba**" etc. The player who manages to form the most sentences in this coded language, wins.

Tips: This game is called "Língua do Pê" in Brazil, and children play it by adding the syllable "pê" before every syllable, for example: *"pêvo pêcê pêquer pêbrin pêcar"* = *"Você que brincar?"* = *Do you want to play?* Every language has different syllables to use as a "code" in this game. Let your children discover how this game is played in all their languages. To increase the challenge, each player can speak in another language (that all players understand!). Another side effect of playing this game in an additional language is that your children will learn its syllable structure.

45. Can you count until 100?

Age group: 10+

Description: You take turns in counting up to 100 as fast as you can. Players agree on whatever number they want to avoid before starting.

For example, you can decide that all numbers that can be divided by 6 or that contain a 6 need to be avoided and the player has to say "oops" (or another word of your choice). You can also agree on skipping that number and say the next following number instead.

You can also opt to combine numbers, for example, that the numbers from 1 to 100 don't have to be divisible by 4 and 7, and not contain either of the numbers etc., and that players who would be supposed to say these numbers should say *ping* if the number contains 4 or can be divided by 4, and *pong* if the number contains a 7 or can be divided by 7.

Tips: Choose the numbers and multiples of numbers that your children know or are learning the time tables from. If your children are not schooled in one of your family languages, they might need some time and support to learn the numbers. Especially children who are schooled in a language like English where numbers are said from left to right — *thirty-nine* — switching to a language like German, where most two digit numbers are said from right to left — *39 neun-und-dreißig* (9 — 30)— requires some training to get it right. Also, languages like French, with 89 *quatre-*

vingt-neuf (4—20—9) can be challenging for children who are not consistently using them. You may not want to rush the players.

46. Long Sentence — Memory game

Age group: 10+

Description: The first player starts a sentence with one word, like "playing". The next player repeats this word and adds another one, like "playing football". Every following player repeats the former sentence and adds another word — like "playing football is…". Every word counts, also "the, of, from, at…". The game ends when someone makes a mistake.

Tips: You can play this game in all your family languages. Depending on the age and language fluency of the players, you can use more complex sentence structures, with subordinates for example: "Peter, my brother, who likes skating, ate an apple with a cinnamon roll, while laying on a long chair that was standing on the balcony of his fathers' aunt Mary….". Younger children would add one word at a time, older ones or adults would add "article + noun" (*the+car*) or entire subordinates, like in the example above: *who likes skating*.

47. Fight for attention

Age group: 12+

Description: You assign a topic to two players. After a short preparation, both players need to talk about this topic with the other group members for 2 minutes each. The group then decides whose talk was more interesting and why.

The children should choose topics they are familiar with, have learned about, or read a book about, or let one of the other participants decide the topic.

Tips: If the language chosen for this activity is not the most dominant one for the children, allow them to prepare for it, maybe write down some words and use a dictionary.

The aim of this game is not to produce a perfect speech or win a debate, but to become confident in speaking about a topic and express thoughts in a captivating (or convincing) way.

48. Association — Meaning game

Age group: 12+

Description: This game is all about being spontaneous and quick. Players are prompted by words like "cow". The next player needs to say a word that can be associated with "cow", like "milk", the third player could then say "white", the forth "snow" and so on. The player that takes longer than the agreed time to find a word, has to wait for the next round to play.

One rule can be to avoid verbs or adjectives, or names of animals, plants etc. to make it more difficult.

Due to the speed and the concentration required by the players, make sure that you keep the fun factor throughout the game.

Tips: If players struggle with finding words or with concentration, you may want to skip the time factor and focus on finding words, allowing players to help each other or use a dictionary.

49. Listen… — Find Word Patterns

Age group: 12+

Material: a chair / a drawn line

Description: Players stand behind a line, a few meters away from a goal (it can be a chair set up in the middle of the room).

The first player chooses a word that the other players will need to guess and starts talking, repeating this word in sentences that she makes up. She can tell a story around the word or hide the word in other words.

The other players who stand behind the line, know that this word can be hidden in other words.

For example "car":

> *There are many **car**s on the street these days. Do you know that my sister has a s**car** on her leg? The other day she put on a lot of mas**car**a and my mother scolded her for that. My brother, Os**car**, told me that he got a good grade today. Luckily he didn't get dis**car**ded from his team! …*

If a player thinks to have recognized the word, he runs to the goal. Is it the right word, he wins and gets to choose the next word and start the game over.

If the guessed word was not the right one, he needs to "pay" by doing an activity (like jumping on a leg around the table; clapping hands etc.)

Instead of the activities to do if a player doesn't guess the right word, you can let him "pay" with a pebble or a card.

You can play this game in two teams. The team that guesses more words wins.

Tips: If the players find it too difficult to find a series of words that contain the same word, you can let them consult an online word generator in the language of the game.

50. Composing your own rap

Age group: 12+

Material: music, rap, dictionary, smartphone or camera

Description: This activity aims at composing a rap — or any kind of song that appeals to your children — and recording it. To start with, your children can take the lyrics of a song they like and change some words of it to make it funny or to change it completely.

Tips: Your children can use all their languages, either combine them in one song, or choose to re-write a song in another language, or use gibberish to make it funnier. Rap is appealing to many preteens and teens, as its rhythm allows to accentuate syllables, sometimes in an unusual way.

If played in groups, each player can provide a few sentences of the rap, write them down, and the group can combine them to form a song. It can but it doesn't need to make sense, the main focus should be on the pleasure to play with sounds, intonations, words and their meanings. For children who are old enough to have a social media account, they can post the recorded song there, making sure that everyone involved agrees! — There are many filters that can alter faces or even voices, so let your teenagers play with it!

51. Guess the language

Age: 12+

Description: This is a game that allows multilingual children to play with all kinds of accents, the ones of their family languages, community languages: any language they want. The aim is to play with accents and intonations and let others guess what language you're imitating. It is not about using words of the other language, but about focusing on the accentuation of words, the intonation, and other particularities and details, like gestures for example. — To get inspired you can search for "foreign accents" on Youtube.

As accents are often used to discriminate, make sure that nobody feels judged or hurt by exaggerating an accent.

Before picking up a book or a pencil...

Before children start learning to read and write, they must learn so much about language — its sounds, rhythm, words and their meanings, structure, purpose, the give and take of conversation, among other things. **Oral language lays the foundation for reading and writing skills.** And it's all learnt through observation, imitation and experimentation. Children need a lot of language input and interaction in order to learn to speak. Multilingual children even more so! Make sure you experiment with a variety of speaking activities from the previous section.

52. Read aloud

Age group: any

Material: books, ebooks, magazines

Description: We are sure you have heard all about the benefits and importance of reading aloud to your children since they are babies. It builds vocabulary, knowledge of the world, creativity, and it helps you bond. But not all read-alouds are the same. Children learn best when the experience is engaging, memorable, filled with emotion. So, even though you might be reading the same picture book for the umpteenth time, put your heart into it!

If you make reading aloud a habit in your family, you will all benefit from it even when your children are already independent readers. Sharing what we read helps to foster vocabulary in our family languages, connection with our dear ones and hones their oral language skills — how to structure an argument, how to voice an opinion etc.

Tips: Read as often as possible. Anywhere, anytime that works for you. Let your child choose the book. Try to read with rhythm and intonation, making voices and sounds.

Interact with your children while reading, answer their questions, ask more questions, comment on pictures. Connect what you read to real life, to what they know, and don't worry about finishing a book. Put it aside if your child is not engaged at that moment.

53. I spy...

Age group: 3+

Description: Look around and choose one thing you can see. Say, "I spy with my little eye something that starts (or ends) with /sound/". Your child has to look around and find what you see. Take turns.

Examples: "I spy with my little eye something that starts with /f/". "Flowers!"

"I spy with my little eye something that ends with /n/". "Crayon".

Tips: You can also play this with rhymes. Example: "I spy with my little eye something that rhymes with fox". "Socks!" You can also play it with colours, shapes, textures etc.

54. Sorting Letter/Sounds

Age group: 3+

Material: small objects from around the house or pictures, scissors, glue and paper

Description:

Objects — decide on two or three letters/sounds to work with. Choose a spot for each letter/sound (on the table, on the floor, on the mat, for example). With your child, go around the house picking random (small) objects. Let's say you chose /t/, /s/, /b/. Then you go and collect a **b**ook, a pencil*, **s**cissors, a **t**eddy **b**ear, a **b**all, a car*, a **b**lanket, a **b**ox, a hat*, **s**ocks and more. Let your child say the name of the object aloud and tell you what the first sound of that word is. Help your child place each object in the chosen spot according to their initial sound. Some objects will not be sorted, since their names don't start with the chosen sounds (like the ones we indicated with an *).

Pictures — Take some old magazines, catalogues or newspapers, scissors, glue and sheets of paper (your choice of size and colour).

Decide on a letter/sound (only one per page) and search for pictures of things that start with that sound. Glue them on the page, write the letter/sound on the top and that's it! You can hang it on the fridge, on your child's bedroom walls or you could gradually make a sound-picture book.

Tips: If the initial sounds for an object or a picture vary in the other language, you can make two lists or two groups, one for each language.

55. Rhyming Sentences

Age group: 5+

Description: Prompt your children with sentence starters that they have to finish with a rhyme.

Examples:

There's a boy called **Jack** who lives in a ____ (a word that rhymes with *Jack*).

Have you ever seen a **cow** ____ (a word that rhymes with *cow*)?

Tips: If coming up with your own sentences is hard, you can use rhyming sentences from nursery rhymes, songs or children's books.

56. Making up characters

Age group: 5+

Description: Invite your child to help you make up a character for a story. All his/her answers have to start with the same letter-sound.

Examples:

What's your name? Matt.

Where are you from? Madagascar.

What's your favorite food? Mashed potatoes.

What are your hobbies? Music and Minecraft.

Who are your best friends? Mary and Max.

Do you have a pet? Yes, a monkey!

Tips: Create a story about your character! You can just tell it orally, with pictures only or eventually write it. You can create a video or perform a play to the rest of the family, friends or pets!

57. Odd one out

Age group: 5+

Description: Say three words, two of which rhyme. Your children have to choose the one that doesn't. **Examples:** You say *dog, jog, mud*. They have to say that *mud* doesn't rhyme.

Tips: Try it with longer words, with bigger groups of words, with pictures or objects, whatever feels right for you. You can also play this with focus on initial sounds. Try to play it in all the languages you speak at home.

58. Tongue Twisters

Age group: 5+

Description: Tongue twisters use alliteration and are great to promote awareness of how the sounds of your language are articulated. They are funny and often tricky to say. Try learning some with your child and challenge yourselves to say them as fast as you can and as many times as you can.

The most popular tongue twister in English is probably "*She sells seashells by the seashore.*" How about in your language(s)?

Tips: If you don't speak or are learning the other family language or the majority/environment language, ask your kids to teach you some tongue twisters they know. You will sure have a laugh together!

59. Word Puzzle

Age group: 6+

Description: Think of a word. Divide it into syllables. Say them in a mixed order. Your child has to arrange them in order to make the correct word. For example: you say *me-ter-lon-wa*; your child has to figure out the word *watermelon*.

Tips: Adapt the length of words to your child's age and ability to recognize syllables. If your children can already read, you can write down the different syllables.

Alternatively, you can create actual puzzles, dominoes or memory games with words broken down into syllables.

60. Word Snake

Age group: 6+ or if your children are confident in distinguishing the sounds

Material: none (or writing material)

Description: You can do this orally or write it down in the shape of a snake. You start with a word, let's say *top*. Your child has to add a word that starts with the last sound of the previous one, /p/. Your snake might look like: *top pet tin nap pack Karen nut tennis Sunday*... If you can't come up with a word, you're out. The game ends when there are two participants left and one of them can't come up with a word.

Tips: Challenge your kids to create the longest snake (on a big piece of paper, board, or on the ground)! Time the game until it comes to a halt. Try to beat your own time vs number of words.

You can play this game in all your languages, and older children might choose to play it by alternating languages. An alternative is to ask participants to form sentences with the word snake where the word order follows the grammatical order in the target language, for example *Tom makes small letter rolls*.

Supporting motor skills development

61. Cooking

Age group: 2+

Material: cooking ingredients and kitchen utensils

Description: Depending on your children's age, they can help you prepare a recipe by mixing, stirring, chopping, peeling, shredding, sprinkling, kneading, decorating. A fun and delicious way to foster vocabulary and fine motor skills. Talk about what you are doing, name things and actions, describe what you see, hear, touch, smell, taste.

Tips: Make sure your children are working with utensils that are safe for them and at a safe distance from heat. Show them how to do something and let them try, but avoid taking over. Older children can read the recipe for you.

You can also introduce concepts like quantities and measuring, which will introduce basic skills in maths. Sharing a family recipe or a traditional dish from your country is a wonderful way to bond and create affective memories with their heritage cultures and languages.

62. Building

Age group: 2+

Material: wooden blocks, plastic bricks, natural materials, things from around the house, recycling materials (eg. cartons, toilet paper tubes, bottle caps, boxes, popsicle sticks, jars, etc.)

Description: Building is not only a physical activity that helps develop motor skills, but a way to engage in creative, imaginative play and storytelling. You and your children can build tents, forts, bridges, castles, huts, prisons, stores, spaceships and so much more!

Tips: Talk about what you are doing and engage with your children's imaginative play. Show them how to do something (stacking, cutting, glueing, etc.) and let them try. Make sure you use a great range of vocabulary related to the activity. With older children you can expand terms they already know, help them find synonyms (eg. *glue*, *stick*, *fix*, *cement*) and use terms in your family language that they might already use in their school language.

63. Crafts

Age group: 2+

Material: natural materials, recycling materials, different types of paper, paint, pencils, crayons, markers, glue, scissors, beads, buttons, cotton balls, wool, clay etc.

Description: Search online for specific craft ideas: holidays you celebrate, seasons, favorite book or movie, occasion cards, origami, diy gifts, a topic they've been learning at school or are particularly interested in.

Tips: Depending on your children's ages and interests, you can create lovely crafts that will not only entertain them, but also develop fine motor skills, creativity and oral language. Name and describe the materials you are using. Talk about the steps you're following, what you need to do next and so on. Ask your children what they think of the result and of the process (which part was tricky to do? Which one was fun?).

64. Drawing and colouring

Age group: 2+

Material: paper, pencils, crayons, pens, paint, chalk, board, pavement

Description: Have a drawing space and materials available for your children to explore. Avoid expecting 'results'. Depending on your children's age, they will scribble, begin to draw random lines and shapes, then more recognizable objects and people. Drawing helps the development of fine motor skills, hand-eye coordination, concentration, creativity and more. And there is usually a description or story behind it, so listen carefully!

Tips: You can search online for drawing activities by age or topic. Do some shared drawing — alternate between you and your child adding a small part of a picture. Older children might enjoy video or book tutorials on how to draw specific things. Choose a place to keep or display their best work. You can also turn your children's drawings into posters, jewelry, clothing, puzzles, pillows, mugs, tote bags, stuffed animals, books, occasion cards, etc.

Learning to Read and Write

Learning to read and to write is a complex process that requires **time, practice and lots of patience.** Unlike learning to speak, it doesn't happen naturally — it needs **explicit teaching.**
The good thing is, once children learn the mechanics of reading and writing — **a code of symbols that represent words** — they should be able to use those basic skills in any other language.
However, **your family's unique situation** will determine the outcomes — the combination of languages and writing systems, the time dedicated to reading and writing in each language, expectations and purpose for learning, your ability to support home learning, your children's ages, motivation and more.

Below are some ideas that might inspire you and help you teach your children to read and write in your family languages. Some can be naturally **blended in your routine**, while others will need more **planning, preparation and follow up**.

Don't be discouraged! You don't have to figure this out on your own. **Reach out to teachers, other parents and other professionals.** Do what you can at home, which starts with providing your children with engaging activities, materials, quality time, patience and lots of love!

Print — making sense of lines and curves

65. Name Crafts

Age group: 3+

Material: natural materials, recycling materials, different types of paper, paint, pencils, crayons, markers, glue, scissors, beads, buttons, cotton balls, wool, clay etc.

Description: Choose your preferred materials and create a poster, object or display with your children's names on.

Tips: If their objects (clothes, backpack, lunchbox) are labelled, point it out and ask them what the label says. Talk about what other words also start with the same letter/sound as their names.

66. Tactile Letters and Numbers

Age group: 3+

Material: magnetic, wooden, foam or sandpaper letters/characters and numbers, stickers, stamps

Description: For younger children this activity is in the spirit of exploration and play. Have the materials available and let them explore. You can guide them to make their names and the ones of other family members. The point is not to learn and name every letter or character, but to become familiar with their shapes.

Older children can be asked to recognize the letters of their names and to make short words.

Tips: Use the tactile letters for sensory play — hide them in a tray with bubbly water, sand, rice, etc. and ask your children to find specific letters or to sort them (by colour, letters that are in your names vs letters that aren't, letters vs numbers).

67. Signs and labels

Age group: 3+

Material: paper, fabric, pens, pencils, markers, crayons, glue, scissors

Description: Depending on your children's age, you can create name labels for their objects (backpack, lunchbox, etc.), a sign for their bedroom door, labels for kitchen/toys/crafts/school storage and organization, and more.

Tips: Point out the labels and signs when you have a chance and ask them or tell them what it says.

68. Letter Hunt

Age group: 3+

Material: none; or paper and pencil, your smartphone or a camera

Description: When you're out and about, invite your children to find specific letters, characters, numbers or words (push, pull, open, closed, stop, entrance, exit, for example) that they recognize.

Tips: If you have more than one child, you can make it a competition. Make a chart or a bingo-like card for each, telling them what they have to look for. Compare the cards when they are done and discuss what they've found, where, etc.

If you have one child, you can challenge yourselves to find more than the previous time you were out letter hunting.

69. Close reading

Age group: 3+

Material: books

Description: As you read together, call your child's attention to certain elements of a book:

The cover: look at the picture and ask what the story is about. Point out the title: "Look, this says ___. It's the name of the story."

Book structure and reading direction: let your children hold the book and turn the pages. They will learn which way is up, which way the book opens and where the story begins and ends.

Letters, words, sentences: when reading together, invite your children to spot letters or numbers that are familiar to them (letters that are in their names, letters or numbers they have begun to learn).

As you read, run your finger under the words. Your children will become familiar with the idea that words on the page correspond to the words you're saying. When you finish reading all the words on that page, it's time to turn it to the next one. They will also learn how your particular language is read (left to right, right to left).

Tips: With older children, point out the difference in fonts, styles, lowercase and uppercase, and clarify that no matter what they look like, the letters remain the same. If your family languages have different scripts, point that out as well.

Children's books often have repetitive, rhythmic, rhyming language. Point out words that have become familiar. Ask your children to find a familiar word or phrase. When you're reading, pause before a rhyme or repetitive word and let your children fill in.

70. Eat them!

Age group: 3+

Material: letter-shaped pasta, cookies, candy, etc.

Description: When eating anything letter-shaped, take the chance to play and talk about it. You can make your names before eating them, pick and eat all the letters (whichever you choose) first. Talk about words that start with those letters or see which letter is tastier.

Tips: Older children can form longer and complex words in all their languages.

71. Environmental Print

Age group: 3+

Material: product packaging or print-outs

Description: Choose products or places that are familiar to your children. Cut out or print their logos. You can make your own memory game, bingo, puzzle, scavenger hunt, guessing game, etc.

Tips: If you have products and print-outs with different languages, you can sort the products or cut-outs by language and explore how many languages you recognize and understand in your family.

72. Calendar/Routine chart

Age group: 3+

Material: a ready-made poster or craft materials for you to make your own

Description: Choose a place in your house where the chart will be visible and accessible to your children at the moments you'll most use them.

Make a calendar with movable cards for the seasons, months, days of the week, numbers, weather. Create a routine of changing the cards together and start talking about the day ahead.

Have a template (weekly or daily) where you can stick the pictures of activities, tasks or chores to be completed that day. This depends on your children's ages and your aim. For example, younger ones might have a reminder of their morning/evening routine: *get dressed, eat, brush teeth, go to the toilet*, etc. Older ones might be working on chores: *make bed*, *put dishes in the dishwasher*, *feed pet*, etc.

Tips: You can find lots of ideas and templates online. Use pictures as well as words on your cards and create this together with your children — discuss your routines and tasks and why their collaboration is important. Older children can make these charts and calendars in the language of their choice.

73. Parent - Child message board

Age group: 4+

Material: writing material of your choice (a chalkboard, a whiteboard, a note on the fridge, corkboard, mirror, door or window)

Description: Exchange small notes among your family. They can be as simple as a heart, a smiley face, "I love you", "Have a great day".

Tips: Encourage your children to respond in either writing or drawing. Avoid correcting the spelling as this activity is meant to encourage communication through messaging. Let your older children choose the language they want to write these messages. They might prefer writing them in more than one language!

Learning the code

74. Letter — Sound Matching

Age group: 5+

Material: letter cards, magnetic letters, paper clip, diy dominoes or memory game

Description: The goal of these activities is to practice letters and sounds recognition. Here are a few suggestions:

A) Letter fishing: make a fishing rod by attaching a paperclip to a stick with a string. Spread the magnetic letters on a surface. Say a sound or letter/character name that your children have to fish for.

B) Move to the letter: make movement cards (walk, run, hop, skip, dance, march, crawl, etc.). Spread letter cards around in a wide circle on the ground and ask your children to pick a movement card at random. Say a letter and your children have to go to that card doing the movement they have picked. Example: *Hop to the F!*

C) Dominoes and Memory Game: see **Word Games** below for how to make your own.

Tips: There are many games that you can adapt or invent to practice letters. What do your children enjoy?

75. Touch and Feel

Age group: 5+

Material: dough, clay, plasticine, pipe cleaners, buttons, beans, cotton balls, etc.

Description: When your children are first learning their letters/characters and numbers, take your time exploring their shape and direction using modelling materials and crafts. Form letters with clay, dough and whatever other material you have available and your children enjoy playing with; you can create letter or name posters by gluing pipe cleaners, cotton balls, beans, etc. on a paper. This way, your children will learn what each letter/character/number looks like in a concrete, tactile way, before they can write it down.

Tips: Search for name and letter crafts online, and talk about the letters — do your children know words that begin with that letter? Have they seen it before? Where? Do some letters look alike? What are the differences?

76. Alphabet Book

Age group: 5+

Material: paper, old magazines or printed pictures, or draw your own with pens, pencils, crayons, paint, etc.

Description: Choose a topic your child is interested in (sports, dinosaurs, plants etc.). Together, create a page for each letter of the alphabet, with a word that starts with that letter and a picture. For instance: *A is for* *athletics. B is for basketball.* Make a fun cover, put all the pages together and you have a book!

Tips: You can make books about different topics. Use different colours and sizes of paper or a different technique for the pictures (drawing, painting, collage, etc.).

Older children can write a short sentence about each word.

You can offer alphabet books as a gift for a friend or family member.

If your family languages have different alphabets, try to find similarities and differences and help your child recognize them.

77. Little Writers

Age group: 6+

Material: a notebook or sheets of paper, pencils, eraser

Description: To introduce a writing practice and habit to your children, we suggest two activities:

A) Diary

Have a special notebook where your children write about their days regularly. Start by talking about their day, what their favorite part was and why, where they went, who they saw, what they did. They can choose one thing and draw a picture. Together, come up with a sentence that describes that picture (orally) and let your children write the sentence independently. Encourage them to try, reminding them of letters and words that they have learned. If a word is too long or complicated, show them how it's spelled. Soon, words such as *today, went, saw, played, school*, etc. will become familiar to them. They will also grow confident in writing simple sentences on their own.

B) Retelling or Creating Stories

Start by brainstorming — Who is your story about? Where does it happen? What happens? Why? When? How does it end?

You can start with creating a storyboard with pictures. It can be as simple as one picture representing the whole story or three pictures representing beginning, middle and end. If your children are up for it, they can draw as many pictures as they want and in the end you put it together like a book. When the pictures are ready, tell the story orally and make sentences to go with each picture. Let your children write independently and remind them of letters and words that they have learned. If a word is too long or complicated, show them how it's spelled. At the end, invite your children to read their story to you.

Tips: Invented spelling is ok and even encouraged and celebrated! It's how your children put their skills into practice. These are not spelling activities, so no need to correct every single word. The goal is to encourage the habit of writing and develop the skills of putting thoughts to paper.

78. Word cards

Age group: 6+

Material: paper, pens, pencil, eraser

Description: The aim of this activity is to provide a memory aid for letters and words your children are learning. All you need is card paper cut into rectangles (the size of playing cards) and pencils.

Type 1: On the front of the card your children write the **letter/sound** they're learning. On the back, they write an **example word** and draw a **picture** to illustrate it.

Examples: You are learning the short vowels in English. On one of the cards they write /a/ on the front, and the word *apple* on the back, highlight the 'a', and draw a picture. Think of possible example words together.

In time you will have a stack of word cards. Review them regularly by asking your children to look at the front of each card and say the letter/sound and example word that is on the back (without looking).

Type 2: Your children write a focus **word** on the card (a focus word can be a tricky word, a high frequency word, a topic word, etc.) They can write it in different ways: one letter of each colour, using stamps, in cursive, etc. Encourage your children to read them as fast as they can; not for the sake of speed, but of automatic recognition.

Tips: Keep the stack of cards in a ziplock bag, box, tin, or put them together with a keyring or string. Make no more than a few cards at once. Review the current stack of cards until reading and spelling are automatic. When a word is learned (reading and spelling consistently accurate) you can put it away. Children of different ages can play this together.

Doing this activity in all your family languages is a good opportunity to highlight the differences in sounds and orthography.

79. Word games

Age group: 6+

Material: paper, pencils, white board, markers

Description: These are quick, easy and fun ways to incorporate spelling practice in your routine. Choose your focus (rhymes, a particular letter/sound, words that begin/end with __, sight words, etc.) and have fun!

A) Hangman

Agree on a category of words that your children are familiar with. Draw the post which the man hangs from. Choose a secret word and draw a horizontal line for each letter. The other player starts guessing letters. If the player is right, write the letter in the correct place. If the player is wrong, draw one part of the man's body and write the letter somewhere else on the page/board.

The game ends when the player gets the word or when the man is fully drawn and hangs.

B) Word Ladder

Start on the bottom of the page or board. Write a word (short, easy to make other words from). Take turns replacing *one letter* of that word in order to create a new one, without adding more letters to the first word. Write that one above the previous one, creating a ladder. **Examples:** man - ma**d** - **p**ad - pa**t** - pe**t** - **b**et - be**d** (and so on).

Tips: You can play this game in all your languages. Depending on your children's fluency, they can alternate between their languages and occasionally add a letter. For example: man – **r**an – *Rad* – rat etc. or: bet – *Beet* – best – **r**est – *reist* (English/*German*).

C) Scavenger Hunt

Make word cards and hide them around the house, or just stick them on the walls.

Instruct your children on which words to find and bring back to you.

Examples: "We're looking for words that have the /t/ sound in them". Or "We're looking for words that rhyme with mat".

Your children have to find all the words that you hid and bring them back to you.

You can time it if it's fun for your children. They can try and beat their own record next time! End it by asking your children to read all the words found.

D) Dominoes

Cut some rectangular pieces of card and draw a line in the middle, widthwise. Choose pairs of matching words, write one in each space, making sure the matching pair is not on the same card.

How to play: Divide the cards equally among players. The youngest player places a card on the table. The game moves on clockwise. The other players take turns checking their cards for the matching one. Players read the word pair as they put their card down.

The player with no more cards in their hands first is the winner.

E) Memory Game

Choose pairs of matching words, cut square pieces of paper (thick or dark, so that it is not see-through) and write one word on each. You can also match words or letters with pictures, for example: on one card you write the letter 'b' and on the other card you draw a banana. **How to play:** Spread all the cards face up on a surface and take a good look. Then turn the cards down and let the youngest player begin. He'll flip two of the cards up and, if they match, take them. If they don't, he'll turn them face down again. The aim of the game is to remember and to gather as many matching pairs as possible.

F) Crosswords and Word Searches

There are different options for Crosswords and Word Searches: there are traditional books you can buy, apps, free printables or you can make your own.

Make sure they are appropriate for your children's language level.

80. Spelling Games

Age group: 6+

Material: *Scrabble Junior*, *My First Bananagrams*, etc., or similar games in your language

Description: Once your children know the letters and are beginning to write short words, these spelling games will support their skills in an informal and fun way.

Pay attention to your children's level and adapt your support by guiding or challenging them when they need it. You can show them how to use a dictionary to find the correct spelling of words.

Tips: If you want to play these games in all your languages, make sure that all the letters and letter combinations are in the set. You can combine your languages in the game, but make sure to agree on the rules before starting; you may have to agree on inventive spelling in words like for example "Schule" (German) and "shoe" (English) for the *sh-* or *sch-*. Encourage your children to come up with rules about spelling in two different languages themselves.

81. Decodable Books

Age group: the age your child starts learning to read, which might vary according to your country's school system or your homeschooling choice.

Material: decodable books/early readers

Description: Decodable books are especially designed for children who are beginning to receive literacy instruction. They should be able to read most of the words *independently*. This promotes a sense of accomplishment and motivation.

Find out what the best series are in your language (check out official education sites from your country, teacher blogs or ask friends who have school-aged children). Incorporate listening to your child read in your routine.

Tips: Be patient! Little readers are sometimes slow or insecure. Let them take their time and reassure them often. You can help by pointing under each letter as your child reads it, then sweeping under the word to signal blending (putting the individual sounds together into a word). If needed, you can quietly whisper the sounds or words, to keep them going.

These stories are usually short and simple. Add some depth by looking at the pictures, asking open questions and connecting it to your own life.

Keep reading books to them that are slightly above their independent level. This adds a richer vocabulary exposure, more interesting stories, deeper topics for conversation and you'll be modelling fluent reading to them.

Celebrate the fact that they can read independently! Experiment with higher levels once your children can read most of the words of the current level on their own.

Publishers often make books available online, so try to get a few for free!

82. Spelling Tricky Words

Age group: 6+

Material: word cards; a tray, salt/sand/rice; magnetic letters; sticky notes; stamps; ziplock bag, hair gel

Description: In English, *sight words* or *tricky words* are the ones children need to recognize by sight, since they can't be decoded sound by sound.

Examples: *the, are, was*. Children will also be encouraged at school to read and spell *High Frequency Words* correctly and automatically, which will contribute to their fluency. Examples in English: *said, because, come*. Find out what *High Frequency* or *Sight words* are in your family languages, and **print a list or make word cards**. Following the list, introduce a few words every week. At school, children are expected to practice these words consistently with the goal of automatization. Once your child can read and spell a word confidently, put the card away and introduce a new one.

Here are six ways to practice reading and spelling this kind of words:

A) Salt Tray

Fill a tray with a layer of salt (alternatively sand or rice).

Put the word cards next to it.

Ask your children to read the card that's on top, spell it in the salt with their finger while saying each letter name, then say the word and shake the tray. It would look like this: "*Said, s-a-i-d, said*". Put that card on the bottom of the stack and proceed to the next one. Keep the salt in a special jar to use again.

B) Magnetic Letters

Spread the magnetic (or wooden) letters on the table, take a word card and let your children read it out loud.

Ask your children to build the word using the letters, while saying each letter name, and then say the word one more time.

After practicing the words of the day this way, take the cards and say the words one by one for your child to build without looking.

C) Letter Hunt

Prepare the words of the day by writing each letter on a sticky note, mixing them up and spreading them around the room.

Sit in one place and hold the word cards with you.

Put one card down and invite your children to read it out loud.

Ask your children to go and find one letter at a time, in the correct order, and bring it back to spell that word.

Once they've got all the sticky note letters, ask them to spell the word out loud and say it one more time, like "*s-a-i-d, said.*"

D) Stamping

Put the word cards of the day on the table.

You can ask your children to read a word and spell it out loud, then write it on a paper using the stamps.

E) Ziplock Gel Bag

Fill a big ziplock bag with hair gel (if the gel is transparent, you can add ink or food colouring).

Put the word cards of the day on the table.

Your children can read the word on top, spell it out loud and then write it on the gel bag with their finger.

Finally, they can spell it out loud one more time.

F) Magic Body Parts

Tell your children to imagine their body parts can write in the air. They can choose: finger, elbow, nose, toes? They can also choose what the words will look like: what colour? What size? Maybe it sparkles or shines? Say each word and ask your children to: repeat it after you, spell it in the air while saying each letter name, say the word one last time, erase it (wipe the air).

Tips: You can also play this game by letting one player trace the word on the other player's hand or back. This player needs to guess what word it is.

You can follow these activities with a dictation, or writing sentences using each of the words practiced. Aim to practice regularly, and to vary the kind of activity. Whenever you are reading and writing together, point out the words you've been learning.

Go through your list, but also add words that pop up in your reading routine or words that your child finds interesting.

Understanding Text

83. Predicting

Age group: 5+

Material: books, worksheets (optional)

Description:

Before reading: look at the book cover and title, ask your children what they think the book is about. Ask questions using *who, where, when, what, how* and *why*.

While reading: When appropriate, pause and ask your children what they think will happen next and *why* they think so. "How do you think this character will react?", "Who do you think will help him?", "What do you think they will find?", "Why do you think so?"

Tips: Older children can make a simple chart where they write a few predictions before reading the book. After reading, they can check which predictions were right and write down what actually happened.

Explain the difference between guessing and predicting. **A prediction is based on information they have and they should be able to explain why they think something will happen.**

If their prediction was right, praise the way they listened and observed carefully. If they were wrong, comment on how their prediction could be possible or not, and why, based on the text.

84. Inferring

Age group: 6+

Material: pictures, videos

Description: Choose some family pictures that your children haven't seen before. As you look through them, ask questions that will encourage your children to *read between the lines, to see beyond the surface*.

Examples: "Why do you think they are dressed like that?", "Oh, aunt Mary is making a strange face on this one, why do you think that is?", "What a beautiful place! What do you think it feels like to be there?", "Can you tell when this picture was taken? Why?"

Tips: Try to incorporate inferring when reading stories, news, school material, also when watching movies, looking at pictures, watching people around. Practice it by asking open questions, especially **why** and **how**.

85. Retelling

Age group: 6+

Material: books, videos, paper, pencil

Description: Help your children retell a story by working on the following:

A) The Question Words:

Who, Where, When, What, Why, and How

You can ask questions and discuss orally or you can create a worksheet that your children fill in before retelling the story.

B) The Beginning - Middle - End

Draw a chart in which your children will write or draw the key facts of each part of the story.

Tips: Talk to your children about their day. Encourage them to describe events, to sequence them, and to connect cause and effect.

When your children have really enjoyed a book, encourage them to tell it to a family member or a friend.

86. World knowledge

Age group: 7+

Material: non-fiction books, magazines, news for kids, videos

Description: Choose material that is appropriate for your children's age and language level.

Before reading or watching, discuss what you already know about that topic.

While reading or watching, make connections to other things you know or have seen before.

After reading or watching, invite your children to list a few new things they have learned; ask them what else they would like to learn about that topic; let them share their opinion and what other topic they would like to read about next.

Tips: When visiting parks, zoos, museums, a new city, etc., explore the environment, the history, or any learning opportunity that you might experience.

Older children can write summaries, fill in worksheets, mind-maps, charts, etc. and work more independently. They can prepare a simple presentation for other family members or friends.

87. Mental Images

Age group: 7+

Material: a book or a text, paper, pens

Description: A big part of understanding a text is creating your own mental pictures, making the words on the page more tangible and making sense of the information.

Here is how you can practice with your children:

A) Choose a short book or text and read it aloud to or with your children. They should listen carefully and not look at any pictures. Ask them to draw what they visualized when listening and to retell what they have listened to.

B) Choose a text without any illustrations. You and your children read the same text, then draw a picture (don't discuss it and don't look at each other's drawing until finished). Show your pictures and talk about what you have read and understood.

88. Summarizing

Age group: 8+

Material: text, highlighter, paper/notebook, pencil, eraser

Description: Choose an appropriate text for your children's age and language level.

Before reading: explore the title, subtitles, pictures, the layout and any other information that stands out. Discuss what you already know about the topic. Explain that while reading your children will look for and highlight **keywords and phrases** (the most important and meaningful information).

While reading: Pause now and then to discuss and check understanding (every sentence or every paragraph, depending on text length and child's level). Prompt your children to decide what the keywords are.

After reading: Ask your children to read the keywords and phrases, and to retell orally what they have read. Finally, invite them to write **a short version** of the text.

89. Word Choice Pockets

Age group: 8+

Material: paper, pens, pencils, glue

Description: Cut some squares of paper roughly the size of a jeans pocket. Glue them on a big sheet of card/poster (bottom and sides, leaving the top open like a pocket). On each pocket, write a very common adjective or verb, such as *good, bad, happy, say, walk*. Place the poster where it's easy to refer to.

When you're reading together and come across words of similar meaning to the ones on the poster, make a word card and add it to the pocket.

Brainstorm together: have other words the same or similar meaning as the word on the pocket? Make a word card and put it in the pocket.

Your children can use this word bank when writing. It encourages them to use a more varied vocabulary.

Tips: Show your children how to search for words of similar meaning by using a thesaurus.

90. Word Web

Age group: 8+

Material: paper, pens, pencils; a website or app.

Description: A word web is a very simple way to expand on concepts and vocabulary.

Write a word in the middle of the page and draw a circle around it. Then, write words related to it and connect them with a line, creating a web.

A word web can be used to brainstorm ideas such as descriptions, multiple meanings, categories of words, concepts and more.

It can also be used to take notes when reading about a topic.

Examples: a descriptive word web for the word *Summer* would contain the words *hot, fun, long, busy, lazy, free…*

Tips: It's important to make the word web neat and easy to read. You can keep it for reference when working on a writing task.

Turning ideas into words

91. Building Sentences

Age group: 6+

Material: paper, pens or building blocks (you can write on or glue cards on)

Description: Together with your children, brainstorm words in the categories: **Who** (people, animals), **Doing What** (verbs), and **Where**. Choose a different colour for each category, make cards and write each word on them. Ask your children to pick one random card from each pile, without looking. Display the three cards and make a sentence using those words. **Example:** *My sister is jumping rope in the garden.*

Tips: You can play this in different ways, with different expectations and outcomes.

Create the sentences orally, write them down or add extra details using *adjectives (describing the person, thing or place)* and *adverbs (describing the action)* or using *because…*

92. Shared Writing

Age group: 6+

Material: paper, pencil, eraser, board, marker

Description: When working on a writing task that could be a little challenging for your children's level, try shared writing.

Discuss the topic and help your children organize their ideas, either orally or using a mind-map. Then, ask your children to tell you exactly what they would like to write. You might need to make suggestions and discuss grammar or word choice. Sentence by sentence, write it down on the board or paper and let your children copy it on their own sheet. After every couple of sentences, ask your children to read aloud what you've got so far and prompt what comes next. When the text is finished, let your children read it aloud and share what they think was done well and what could be improved.

93. Recorded Writing

Age group: 6+

Material: smartphone, tablet or other recording device, paper, pencil, eraser

Description: When working on a writing task, help your children express and organize their ideas orally at first. Then, record the sentences one by one. Next, replay each sentence for your children to write down. Once the text is finished invite your children to read it aloud.

Tips: Depending on your goal with each writing task, you will check spelling, grammar, style, layout, etc. Sometimes the content and the purpose are more important, so you don't need to point out every mistake.

94. Dictation

Age group: 6+

Material: paper and pencil or whiteboard and marker

Description: Depending on what your focus has been for spelling, grammar, vocabulary and writing fluency, use dictation to practice.

You can dictate a list of words, sentences or a paragraph. Make sure to repeat the words if necessary, then check it together. Help your children understand how and why a word is spelled a certain way. When finished, let your children read aloud and then write new sentences using the words they struggled with.

95. Sequencing

Age group: 7+

Material: worksheets, copies of cartoons, short comics, any step-by-step in pictures

Description: Make copies of cartoons or step-by-step instruction pictures, cut them out and mix them. You can also find printable worksheets online. Invite your children to look at each picture and describe what they see. Then, ask them to put them in order. Next, encourage them to make sentences (orally) using the words *First, Then, Next, After that, Finally*. Your children can now glue the pictures in order and write their sentences down.

96. Expanding Sentences

Age group: 7+

Material: worksheets or paper and pencil

Description: Write or dictate a simple sentence, for example: *The girl played.* Ask your children to make it more interesting by adding details. You can prompt them with questions such as: "What can we say about the girl? The little girl? The smart girl? The kind girl?" "How did she play? Happily? Excitedly? Quietly?" "Where did she play?" "What did she play?" "With whom?"

Your children can then write down their new, more interesting sentence.

Example: *The little girl played happily in the living room.*

Tips: Encourage your children to enrich their writing by choosing more interesting words, adding description, adding details. Older children can choose a short text and rewrite it, expanding its sentences. You can also make a game out of it: who can write the longest sentence?

97. Text Puzzle

Age group: 7+

Material: text; recipes, game instructions, how-to's, news, product labels, emails, letters, lyrics, poems, etc.

Description: Choose a text appropriate for your children's age and reading level. Make a copy and cut it in strips (every few lines, or paragraphs). Mix it all up and invite your children to read and order the text.

Tips: You can combine different texts and let your children create a new one.

98. Word Choice

Age group: 8+

Material: a short story or poem, highlighter, paper, pencil, Thesaurus (optional)

Description: Choose a short text that is appropriate for your children's age and level. Make a copy. Your children can read it silently and highlight verbs (actions) and adjectives (descriptions) that could be swapped for a more interesting one. Discuss the words chosen and the better option. Invite your children to rewrite the text using the new words.

Tips: You can combine this activity with **Word Choice Pockets**.

99. Questions and Answers

Age group: 10+

Material: paper, pens

Description: Everyone sits in a circle and writes a question on the paper, folds it so the question can't be read, and passes it on to the person on the right. The next person writes an answer, folds the paper and passes it to the person on the right. This goes on and on, alternating between questions and answers until the paper is fully folded. At the end, everyone unfolds the paper and reads the questions and answers out loud. The answers might not make sense at first, but maybe the players can come up with a solution to make it work. This game is like the French game *cadavre exquis*, where players try to solve a crime. Possible questions are: "what happened?", "who did it?", "what did they do then?" etc.

Tips: If the players have different ages, and some can't write or spell very well yet, they can draw the answers. You can play this game in all family languages and could even alternate the languages between questions and answers. A real language mix!

Working on Fluency

100. Audiobooks

Age group: 5+

Material: CDs, podcasts, YouTube

Description: Listening to audiobooks in your family languages can be a pleasant activity that also models fluent reading. You can listen to them whenever it is suitable for your family: in the car, during meals, at bedtime, in waiting rooms, at bath time, etc.

Talk about the stories with your children: What is their favorite? Why? Do they notice how the narrator makes voices, uses intonation, and shows emotion? Compare narrators and styles.

Tips: Create your own audio stories and share them with friends and family. If your children are not that fluent enough yet to read in their additional language, listening to an audiobook in combination with the written book can help them become more confident readers.

101. Emotions

Age group: 6+

Material: paper, pens

Description: Together with your children, brainstorm as many emotions as you can. Let your children draw the facial expressions on card-sized

pieces of paper. Write down short, random sentences on strips of paper.
Examples: *Yesterday I went to the dentist. / Grandma will bake a cake. / Can you come here?* Each participant takes one sentence and three emotion cards, then reads the same sentence showing the different emotions.

Tips: Play this game in all your family languages and explore how the emotions are described and called in different ways from language to language.

102. Paired Reading

Age group: 6+

Material: books

Description: Choose books that are on your children's reading level or slightly above. Read together, alternating the parts that you read and that they read — every other page, paragraph or line. Model fluent reading by using good intonation, rhythm and making characters' voices. Encourage your children to do the same.

Tips: If your children need a little more modelling and fluency practice, read each page or paragraph aloud and invite them to read it again after you.

Search online for advice on how to find the right book for your children's level.

103. Recorded Reading

Age group: 7+

Material: books or other texts, recording device (smartphone, tablet, laptop)

Description: Choose a text on your children's independent reading level. Let them read it silently first. Then, invite them to read it aloud and record it. Listen to the recording together and discuss positive points and points for improvement with regards to clear pronunciation, pace, phrasing, intonation when reading questions or exclamations, using characters' voices, etc. Ask them to read aloud and record again. Compare. Talk about how practicing reading aloud helps you do it better each time.

Tips: This activity can help children who are learning an additional language to practice their pronunciation and become more confident in speaking.

104. Drama

Age group: 7+

Material: text (short stories with dialogue or plays)

Description: Choose a story that your children love. If necessary rewrite it together so that it is like a short play. Assign the roles of narrator and characters. Read it aloud, each one performing their role. Discuss emotions, voice, intonation. Repeat it a few times and discuss how practicing reading aloud helps you improve.

Tips: You can go as far as performing it with costumes, props, puppets, toys or making a movie or audiobook.

105. Punctuation

Age group: 8+

Material: paper, pens

Description: Choose which punctuation marks you will practice (see list below). Draw each one on a piece of paper and display them on the table or floor. Write down sentences and questions on strips of paper, leaving out the punctuation. To make it more engaging and memorable, write nonsense, funny or exaggerated sentences.

Ask your children to read the sentences aloud and match them to the correct punctuation mark. It can be helpful to choose the ones your children have already learned at school, then practice them in your family language (s). Here's a list of punctuation marks used in English: Full stop (.), Exclamation mark (!), Question mark (?), Comma (,), Speech marks (""), Apostrophe ('), Colon (:), Semicolon (;), Parenthesis (()), Brackets ([]), Dash (—), Hyphen (-), Slash (/), Ellipsis (...).

Tips: You can find printable worksheets to practice different kinds of punctuation and at different levels. When you're reading together, draw your children's attention to punctuation and how to read the sentences properly. Talk about punctuation marks and how they are called and used in all your family languages and explore similarities and differences.

Reading Motivation

106. A Special Treat

Age group: 3+

Material: books

Description: When you buy your children new books — for their birthday, a traditional celebration, a book they've been looking forward to — make it a big deal, make it special. Take them on a date to buy it (bonus: one-on-one time and a yummy treat!). You can make a treasure hunt, or put it under their pillow when they sleep, sneak it in their backpack or toybox. Make it a reward for achieving their reading goals (or other relevant goals), write a heartfelt note on the first page, or wrap it nicely.

107. Reading Dates

Age group: any

Material: books, snacks, picnic blanket, decorations, etc

Description: Create a special moment to read and be cozy.

You can prepare a tasty snack and set the table nicely, or have a picnic in the garden or park nearby. You can also go to a café or cake shop, have hot chocolate in front of the fireplace, or build a fort or tent. Or you designate — and decorate — a reading nook in your house. Go for a bike ride and take a rest break with a book.

Tips: You can make reading a more enjoyable experience by introducing those moments in a very special way. For parents who transmit multiple languages to their children, creating more diverse reading moments in different languages can help to switch to another language. For example, you can designate a space in the living room where you only read German books, another one where you read French books etc. This makes it easier for younger children to make the language switch during reading time.

108. Library visits

Age group: any

Material: your library cards

Description: Go to your local library regularly and explore it together, take your time. Sit at a cozy spot and read. Introduce your children to how a library works, how to ask a librarian for advice, how to borrow a book or as many as are allowed!

Keep an eye on the library's calendar of activities: many have special events like read-alouds, puppet shows, book fairs, book launches etc.

Tips: Some libraries have books in your other languages too. Explore other media like audiobooks, ebooks etc.

109. Organize your bookshelf

Age group: 5+

Material: your books, shelves, boxes, sticky notes

Description: Together with your children, take down all their books and sort them. Let your children re-discover their books and decide which ones they want to keep — even if they have outgrown them! Maybe they would be interested in reading them to younger siblings or friends. Are there books that they don't want to keep anymore? You can donate to a charity, a library, a school, a daycare, or someone you know.

Organize your books so that the spines are visible (on a shelf) or so that they're easy to flip through (in a box). That'll make it easier for them to choose what to read. Place a few books strategically around the house or wherever your kids get bored, like the car.

Notice the types of books you have. Are they mostly fiction or nonfiction? What are they about? Do you have any comics? Any magazines for kids? Any pop-ups or lift-the-flaps? Do you have enough in the minority language?

What are your children's most loved books? Get more of that kind, but also try to add a variety of styles and a balanced mix of languages.

110. Put the books down

Age group: 5+

Material: variable

Description: Sometimes the motivation to read more and to enjoy it will come when you put the books down and become active and creative with the world they represent.

You can create a story-related craft or write an alternative ending to the story together with your children. You can also write a letter to their favourite character or author.

What about making fictional food (like Roald Dahl's BFG's Frobscottle) or story-inspired food, or making a recipe from a cookbook for kids.

Watch a book-based movie together with fresh popcorn, or listen to movie soundtracks or audiobooks.

Tips: When starting any activity inspired by a book, you can invite your children to choose whatever language they prefer. It is interesting to explore what aspects of the book are maintained or changed in a book-based movie.

111. Reading Goals

Age group: 6+

Material: paper, pens, pencils

Description: discuss and decide on your reading goals. Make them realistic and achievable for your children's age, but not too easy.

It's important that you don't impose a goal on your kids. Help them come up with it themselves and they'll have a sense of responsibility over it. A reading goal can be set in time (minutes a day), number of pages, or number of books.

Tips: It can be useful to keep a visual record to help you stay on track. You can choose an appropriate reading log, for example, and pin it on your fridge.

You may discuss and decide what the reward could be once the goals are achieved and how often: daily, weekly or monthly?

You can encourage older children to read similar books in all their languages or to alternate between texts: newspaper, magazine, comics, novel etc. when alternating between languages.

112. Book Swap

Age group: 6+

Material: used books

Description: If you know other families (in your area, at school or virtually) who speak your languages and are passing them on to their children, organize book swaps. You'll enjoy different stories without having to buy new books. Declutter your bookshelf, spark your children's curiosity and foster a sense of community.

In-person book swap party: make a list of participants and books donated. The participants get a token per book brought in, which can be swapped for any other book at the party. Organize the books in your preferred way: by age, genre, language, topic. Make sure the books being swapped are in decent condition. Ask the other parents to help with the organization — collecting tokens, minding children, reading aloud, bringing snacks, etc.

Virtual book swap: social media platforms have groups dedicated to multilingual families where you can reach out and connect to someone who might be interested in swapping books with you and your children. It is easier to swap with someone whose children are about the same age as yours and who share the same language scenario. List the books you're giving out, agree on which ones are getting swapped and post them to each other.

Tips: If you keep regular contact, your children can share their readings, video chat or correspond with each other.

113. Review and Rate

Age group: 8+

Material: internet, laptop, smartphone or tablet

Description: Join free websites where your children can review the books they read, share recommendations and see what other kids are reading. They might also feel motivated by seeing their 'Read' list grow.

114. Join a Book Club

Age group: 9+

Material: books

Description: Find out if there is a book club in your area, in your family language. If there isn't one, could you organize it? What about regular read-alouds/playdates with other families? Another option is to find a virtual book club.

115. Watch Booktubers

Age group: 12+

Material: internet, laptop, smartphone or tablet

Description: *Kid Booktubers* are sharing their genuine love for books on Youtube and Instagram. Watching their reviews and recommendations might be the extra nudge of inspiration for your children.

Writing Motivation

116. Cards

Age group: 5+

Material: cards, envelopes, pens, post stamps

Description: This is a habit you can cultivate, if it suits your family. Have plenty of occasion or blank cards at home. Whenever the opportunity comes up — be it joyful like birthdays, holidays, weddings, travel, births, or sad like illness and death — write a card together. Discuss the occasion and what you'd like to say to the person. Help your children write a simple draft of the message. When you're both happy with the text, ask your children to write it down on the card.

Tips: Writing cards in different languages will help your children not only to understand a formal writing style, but also the culture that is connected with the opportunities they write the cards for.

117. Happiness Jar

Age group: 6+

Material: a jar, tin or box, strips of paper or sticky notes

Description: Take a jar, tin or box. Decorate it with your children, make it special. Occasionally talk about something good that happened, something that made them smile, something that they're grateful for.

Invite them to write it down and put it in the jar, tin or box. After some time you can open it and read the notes together.

Tips: Let your children choose the language they want to write the note in.

118. Toy Stories

Age group: 6+

Material: toys, smartphone (to take pictures), pen, paper

Description: Toys can be fantastic learning tools! You can play together, ask questions, describe, tell stories.

These are suggestions on how to encourage writing while playing with toys:

You can give your children a *writing prompt (easily found online)* and let them build the beginning, middle and end scenes using toys. Encourage them to tell the story orally, or take pictures of the scenes, then write the story together. The amount of support you give will depend on your children's level. Finally, put the pictures and text together as a book or comic story.

You can also observe their play and, when the opportunity comes up, suggest writing a story based on what they are building and playing.

119. Stop Motion Video

Age group: 6+

Material: camera, smartphone or tablet, stop motion software, toys and figurines

Description: *Look for specific instructions on how to create a stop motion video online.*
Let your children choose a story they like, and plan and write the script: describe the scenes and write the characters' lines. Divide the roles and practice reading. Follow the instructions to make the movie and add voiceover.

Tips: Let your children choose the language. They might want to do it in their most dominant language, but could also add some scenes in their other languages, or give characters another language, for example.

120. Read About Authors

Age group: 7+

Material: biographies, blogs, Youtube

Description: Look for biographies, articles, interviews, blogs or videos about your children's favorite authors. Learning more about a writer's life, work and inspiration might motivate your children to appreciate reading and writing even more.

Tips: Take the opportunity to attend live events: read-alouds, signing sessions, workshops or book launches by children's authors and illustrators.

121. Comics

Age group: 7+

Material: paper, pens, pencils or websites and applications

Description: If your children love drawing, take advantage of that and explore creating characters and scenarios. Ask them about characters' traits, where they live, what their favorite things are, what kind of adventures they would go on. Discuss the characteristics of a comic story: the format, the length, the language.

You can choose different levels of support:

– Invite them to tell you the story orally first.

– Write the story yourself and encourage your children to illustrate it.

– Let them illustrate the story and then write it together.

– Encourage them to create everything — writing and pictures.

Tips: If this is something that your children really enjoy doing, create a portfolio or put the stories together in a book. Ask them if they'd like to share it somehow: send a copy to family and friends, on a blog, social media or at school.

122. Snail Mail

Age group: 7+

Material: paper, pens, envelopes, post stamps

Description: Together with your children, write letters or cards to friends and family and mail them. Let them know that you would love to get a response (to keep your children motivated).

Tips: Discuss the idea of having a pen pal to correspond in the minority language. If your children are on board, search for one in online groups for multilingual families.

123. Journal or Scrapbook

Age group: 7+

Material: a notebook, pencils, pens

Description: Encourage your children to keep a journal or scrapbook. Help them decide what they would like to write about frequently. Remind them to write in it when you notice something worth journaling about.

Tips: Your children can keep different types of journals: holidays, trips, outdoors exploration, reporting outings, special occasions, book reviews, game reviews, dream journal, learning journal or other topics they love. You can find some journals for sale, with prompts to fill in.

THANK YOU!

We hope that your family enjoys these activities and that they contribute to fostering your children's language skills in the many phases of their language development.

Learning languages is a lifelong journey. We wish you and your family all the passion, resilience, motivation and positivity that it requires.

We would love to hear from you!
Please share your success stories, struggles and questions with us: info@UtesInternationalLounge.com and / or anaelisasm@gmail.com .

You can also find articles and downloadable material related to this *Toolbox* on our websites www.utesinternationallounge.com and www.anaelisamiranda.com.

If this book has been useful to you, please let others know about it! Leave a review on Amazon or share it on social media.

Printed in Great Britain
by Amazon